EDITORIAL AND POLITICAL CARTOONING

EDITORIAL AND POLITICAL CARTOONING

From earliest times to the present
With over 700 examples from the works of the
world's greatest cartoonists

SYD HOFF

STRAVON EDUCATIONAL PRESS
New York

ABOUT THE ORGANIZATION OF THE BOOK

Editorial and Political Cartooning is arranged in three sections. The first, THE OLD MASTERS, is a sampler of the works of some of the outstanding caricaturists and cartoonists from the earliest times to the middle of the 20th century. With the exception of the review of caricature in the early civilizations and through the middle ages, the presentation is loosely chronological by artist. In a few instances cartoons depicting a specific historical event are introduced as a unit and placed in approximate chronological order between the works of cartoonists who were active at that particular time. Examples are "The French Revolution," "The U.S. Civil War," and, "The Spanish American War." On the other hand, the more general topics, "Women's Rights," "War Cartoons," and "Advice and Consent" are, like an addendum, placed at the back of the section.

The second and largest section, THE MODERNS/ UNITED STATES AND CANADA, is arranged, in alphabetical order, by artist.

The third section, THE MODERNS/THE WORLD, is arranged by geographic region and then in alphabetical order by country.

Library of Congress Cataloging in Publication Data
Hoff, Syd, 1912-
    Editorial and political cartooning.
    Includes index.
    1. Editorial cartoons—History. 2. World politics
    Caricatures and cartoons— History. I. Title.
NC1325.H63   741.5'909   75-45314
ISBN 0-87396-078-5

Manufactured in the United States of America

CONTENTS

Preface

RESEARCHERS OF FUTURE BOOKS OF THIS NATURE will find that my *modus operandi* did not substantially lighten their burden, because in researching the material for *Editorial and Political Cartooning*, everything just seemed to fall into place from the very beginning. However, I do recall running around in circles for a while, feeling somewhat like a man chasing butterflies with a hole in his net.

It began with several rolls of stamps and the vague hope that certain artists I had never actually met would take a minute of their valuable time to let me know if a book containing some of their work would be possible. The response was amazing! Every day's mail brought drawings, clippings, confessions. The only rub was that some of these people (certainly older than myself!) claimed to remember me as one of their childhood favorites.

To assemble a representative list of "ancients," several avenues were pursued, specifically libraries, museums and private collections. On the eve of a cataract operation, with only half an eye in working order, I had to apologize to a lady in charge of the Rare Books room at the New York Public Library for making her read to me, and to thank dozens of other persons there for not stepping on me when I fell off a ladder.

For the foreign cartoons I wish to extend thanks to Paulette Segal of the publishers staff, without whose beguiling ways I'm certain a custodian at the United Nations would never have given us access to day-old copies of newspapers from all over the globe. Several other people deserve thanks for helping in compiling foreign cartoons. Especially deserving of acknowledgement are Eleanor D. Worley of *Atlas World Press Review* and Sylvia Roth of Rothco Cartoons, Inc.

Thousands of apologies are due to those artists (and their admirers) whose work either has not been included in the book, or has not been represented more fully. To all of them I can only apologize and say I'm sorry. Certainly, I should have included Daumier's "Will The Eclipse Be Total?"—the 1871 drawing in which a Prussian spiked helmet held up in the sky, obliterates the sun ("Liberty") and casts a shadow over all of Europe; or his "Peace—an Idyl," the French master's conception of the Bonaparte eagle plunging its bloodied beak into the vitals of France, portrayed as Prometheus bound to a rock; and "Equilibre European," in which this hapless planet is held aloft by bayonets in the hands of men of many nations and would certainly fall to its doom should one of them move.

Too, those who worship the Cruikshanks, George, Isaac and Robert, will want me pilloried for not at least remembering George's "The Bank Note Not To Be Imitated," an inspiration perhaps to would-be counterfeiters of the day, but also to other satirists a hundred years later; and "Every Man On His Perch, or Going To The Fair," showing the first cartoon character taking a ride on a cannon, I believe; or "A Chapter On Noses," to this day a lesson in what can be done, artistically, with the human proboscis.

Yes, they will all holler: devotees of Boardman Robinson, because I have omitted his "Death The Reaper," that masterful drawing of the Grim Reaper holding a scythe in a field, addressing Kaiser Wilhelm as a farmer, similarly armed, "Plagiarist! You are stealing my business!"—those who feel cheated because they can't find more of Art Young, maybe one of those that led to his arrest along with the editors of the *Masses*, for opposing American participation in World War I,—those who'll want more Tenniel, Davenport, . . .and they'll be asking: Where is George Grosz who satirized pre-Nazi Germany with drawings revealing such bestial cruelty and decadence, and that led to his fleeing his native country and emigrating to America. Where is Kathe Kollwitz, famous today in fine art galleries for her tender illustrations of war-widowed mothers clutching their young, but also remembered for some like "Never Again War!"—a forceful poster for a Berlin youth rally in 1924? Where are a hundred others?

To all these critics and zealots, again I apologize and humbly beg to be forgiven, but I feel that some explanation is in order. Actually, the reasons are varied, but the ones that probably were decisive include lack of space, inability to get reprint permission, the condition of available prints being unsuitable for reproduction, and material arriving too late to meet the publication deadline.

Gratitude must also be expressed to the following: Alison Dodd of the Swann Collection of Caricatures and Cartoons; Mrs. William P. Banning, daughter of Rollin Kirby; Rick Alley, son and grandson of J. P. and Cal Alley; Frank Spangler, Jr.; Mary Taylor Schilling of Transworld Features Syndicate; and last but not least, for all-around information and an unlimited patience with me, to Draper Hill, of the *Commercial Appeal*, president of the American Society of Editorial Cartoonists and an outstanding member of his profession.

Acknowledgements

Credit is hereby acknowledged and given to the publications and organizations listed below for materials in *Editorial And Political Cartooning*. Other credits are acknowledged throughout the book, either in the author's text or as "credit lines" next to each cartoon. All the cartoons in the section THE MODERNS/UNITED STATES AND CANADA were received from the artists or their representatives. The following are acknowledged: *An Historical Sketch Of The Art of Caricaturing* by J. P. Malcolm, (Langman, Hurst, Recs, Orme, and Brown, 1813), for pages 16, 17, 18, 26, 30; *Caricature And Other Comic Art* by James Parton, (Harper & Brothers, Publishers, 1877), for pages 19, 20, 21, 22, 23, 24, 25, 27, 28, 29, 31, 32, 33, 34, 35, 36, 41b, 44t; *The Comic History of England* by Gilbert Abbott A'Beckett, illustrated by John Leech, (Bradbury, Agnew, & Co.), for pages 42, 43, 44b; *Harper's Weekly* (various issues), for pages 53, 54, 55, 56, 57, 58, 59, 60, 66, 68, 69, 71, 72, 73, 74, 75, 76, 77, 78, 79, 80, 81, 82, 83, 91, 92; *The Southern Illustrated News* (various issues), for pages 62, 63, 64, 65; *Frank Leslie's Illustrated Newspaper*, for pages 84, 85, 86, 87, 88, 89, 90; The Swann Collection of Caricatures And Cartoons, for pages 37, 39, 70; *Atlas World Press Review*, for pages 352, 353, 357, 358, 359b, 374, 375, 376, 379b, 380b, 381, 388t, 389, 391b, 399, 402, 403, 405t, 406, 410br, 412t, 414b; Rothco Cartoons Inc., for pages 354, 359t, 362, 363, 364, 365, 366, 367, 368, 369, 370, 371, 372, 373, 377, 378, 401, 408, 411, 412b, 413.

For inspiration, for ideas, and for sources many books were consulted including the following: Barbara Gelb, *So Short A time*, (1973); Draper Hill, *The Lively Art of J.P.Alley*, (1973); Draper Hill, *Illingworth on Target*, (1970); Draper Hill, *Mr. Gilray, The Caricaturist*, (1965); Draper Hill, *Fashionable Contrasts*, (1966); *Cartoons by Honoré Daumier*, (De Witt Publishing House, 1898); Frederick Burr Opper, *Willie And His Papa.* (1901); *Cartoons of the War of 1898 with Spain*, (Bedford, Middlebrook, 1898); Alfred Connable and Edward Silberfarb, *Tigers of Tammany*, (1967); August L. Freund, *William Gropper, Retrospective*, (1968); *Harper's Encyclopedia of Art*; *McGraw-Hill Dictionary of Art*; Paul Szep, *At This Point In Time*, (1973); *The East is Red*, (People's Press,

1972); Merle Randolph Tingley, *25 Years In An Inkwell*, (1973); Bruce Shanks, *Cartoon Review of '72*, (1972); *Vision Magazine*, (Community Publishing Co. 1973); Doug Wright, *Editorial Cartoons*, (1973); Bob Chambers, *"It's Oil!" and Other Cartoons*, (1972); Edd Ulushak, *The World of Uluschak*, (1973); Art Young, *Art Young's Inferno;* Herbert Block, *The Herblock Book*, (1952); Stephen Hess, *The Ungentlemanly Art*, (1968); Rollin Kirby, *Highlights; A Cartoon History of the 1920's*, (1920); C. L. Bartholomew, *Cartoons of the Spanish American War*, (1899); *The Dollar or The Man*, (Small, Maynard & Co. 1900).

t = top of page; b = bottom of page; l = left side of page; r = right side of page.

Introduction

Mᴏʀᴇ ᴛʜᴀɴ 20 ʏᴇᴀʀs ᴀɢᴏ ᴀ ᴄᴀʀᴛᴏᴏɴɪsᴛ ᴡʀᴏᴛᴇ ᴛʜᴇsᴇ ᴡᴏʀᴅs: "Everybody can love a comic artist. Not everybody can love a political cartoonist. If you want to be loved by everybody, don't become a political cartoonist." Those sentiments were offered by none other than Syd Hoff—me! And I followed my own advice. I stuck to the comic side of cartooning for all these years, except for a stretch way back in the early days of Hitler's rise to power, when I dabbled in drawings similar to some in this book, and offered them anywhere they would be accepted.

Meanwhile, as fortune smiled on my comic art, I faced the fact that I could not play on readers' emotions day after day, week after week, causing them to feel shock, fear, anger, amusement, despair, and moral indignation, so that they might want to take to the streets, brandish placards, and maybe march on Washington. But there were cartoonists who could keep the editorial and news pages full of exciting and inciting pictures. In fact, ever since the first cartoonist used a pencil or a brush, there have been some who had what it takes to produce this kind of art. It takes not only courage, but also special kind of skill. The courage is needed because there are always some readers who will be offended by the point of view of an editorial cartoon and will demand the job and maybe the hide of the artist. The skill is demanded because it takes a superior craftsman to portray the likeness of the heroes and villains who strut their stuff on the events of the day. A great artist will show the very essence of his subject, and he will make Boss Tweed and Teddy Roosevelt and Chamberlain with his umbrella and Churchill with his cigar remembered through drawings long after words in the editorial and news columns have been forgotten. Some of us are famous through Mickey Mouse and Little Orphan Annie, others through Uncle Sam and John Bull and the elephant and donkey.

As for me, there are days when success as a comic artist is not enough. The urge to do battle with evil becomes irresistible and the Walter Mitty in me takes over. I yearn to follow in the tradition of Daumier and Nast and their worthy descendants whose pictures fill the pages of this book. With a large letter "S" (for Supercartoonist) emblazoned on my chest and a camelhair brush in my hand, I leap tall buildings and lay out crooks, corrupters, and warmongers. Sheer fantasy! But I can and did collect the supercartoons of this and other continents, in these and other times, because I think you will share some of this joy in this special kind of cartooning. I have not restricted my selections to any point of view, and you must remember that whether you approve of the point of view of a cartoon or not, it is still possible to appreciate the art and the skill of the cartoonist. I try to tell you something about the story that goes with these drawings and sometimes point out why one drawing or another is especially effective in getting across a point of view.

I am grateful to each of the artists, who made this book possible. With their indulgence I herewith reprint one of my own drawings, just to get into the act! Now the book is waiting, dear reader; enjoy it as much as possible.

SYD HOFF

"Wow! Now I can decide whether to destroy the world or save mankind!"

"I'm glad Walter Lippmann can't draw."
                —Lyndon B. Johnson

THE OLD MASTERS

The Old Masters

GOD, IT IS SAID, CREATED MAN IN HIS OWN IMAGE. But as soon as the job was finished, many may have thought it should have been done differently.

Whatever early man's motives in caricaturing himself, whether to challenge the wisdom of the Creator or to frighten away evil spirits, it became one of his favorite hobbies and remained with him down through the ages. Eventually it became the medium of social criticism called political cartooning.

Thus, all present-day cartoons and caricatures have their roots in what the primitives did many thousands of years ago. Even then, society was ridiculed or glorified by those pioneer satirists. We see proof of this in

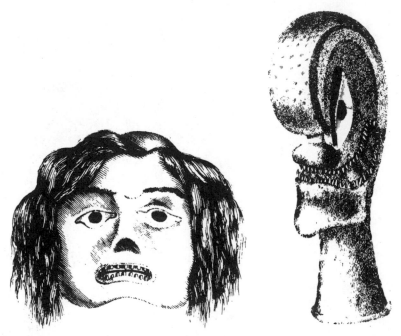

Facsimiles of drawings appearing in *An Historical Sketch Of The Art Of Caricaturing* by J. P. Malcolm, published 1813 and based upon carvings, figures, sculpture, and masks in the British Museum.

16

the most ancient stone chiseling or wood carving, wherever those who look for this sort of thing have struck pick into rock and shovel into earth—kings and chiefs who look ridiculous or magnificent, slaves and commoners who appear crushed or alert. Indeed, it is as though someone had already laid down the ground rules for political cartooning, or as if a kind of international school for comic art was already in operation.

THE CHINESE

To outsiders the Chinese may seem inscrutable, but privately, as we can see by these delightful figures, they are not that way at all. Observe, in particular, the two gentlemen seated below, one tickling his Eustachian tube with an object, the other pouring liquid—lukewarm, presumably—on his tummy.

The lesson from this, perhaps, is that political cartoonists, as well as the rest of us, must disregard popular conceptions about a people, and find out what they're *really* like.

Facsimiles of drawings appearing in *An Historical Sketch Of The Art Of Caricaturing* by J. P. Malcolm, published 1813 and based upon carvings, figures, sculpture, and masks in the British Museum.

THE EGYPTIANS

Three civilizations have left us a distinct heritage of cartooning and caricature: the Egyptian, the Greek, and the Roman. This is perfectly natural, because the history of each is steeped in war, conquest, and brutal tyranny, and where such things exist, artists, sensitive souls that they are, invariably react.

In the case of the Egyptians, we may be surprised, after the majesty and awe of such imposing statuary as Khephren, Ramses, and the magnificent figures like the hippopotamus goddess Thoueris (who watches over pregnant women), to find the comic touch on, of all places, the sarcophagi, stone coffins made into the shape of mummies.

A high priest-fox offering booty to a king-lion, copied from a limestone slab and done about three thousand years ago. (For our purposes, let us observe the very clever animal/human masquerade.)

More Egyptian cartoon-type art, found on tombs and monuments and possibly done "while under the influence." (Wine making was one of the principal activities of the day, from vineyard to vat, and beer, according to authorities, actually had its humble beginning in the land of the Nile.)

Dog-headed monkeys compose the captain and crew on this fateful journey.

"Servants Carrying Their Masters Home After a Night on the Town" (proof of the malt and hops problem mentioned above).

The maid wasn't fast enough when madame imbibed a little more than she could hold.

Two of these plates are noteworthy, at least for providing us with an understanding of ancient Egyptian drinking habits.

THE GREEKS

Famous as "the cradle of civilization," Greece, led by her philosophers, Socrates and Plato, became the greatest think-tank in the history of the world. But like Aristophanes, the immortal playright who satirized not only prominent personalities in public and private life but even the Olympian gods, Greek cartoonists and caricaturists used their art to satirize mythology itself, perhaps because they viewed any attempt to explain various phenomena without material foundation as misleading and inadequate. And so, burlesques of gods and goddesses became the subject of humor, as seen in these drawings copied from ancient Greek pottery.

Reading from right to left: Apollo as a quack doctor on a platform, with old blind Chiron struggling up the steps to consult him, aided by a friend; the nymphs watching from the heights of Parnassus; and the manager of the spectacle looking on from below.

Both of these drawings are done in anything but classic Greek style!

THE ROMANS

No less bold were Roman satirists of a slightly later period who, while their country was engaged in protecting itself from the Teutons in the North, and holding onto Greece in the East, were sculpting "political cartoons" of the day in bas-reliefs such as the Marcus Aurelius Column in Rome, or surreptitiously scribbling them on the walls of Pompeii, a city destined to be buried under an avalanche of molten lava from Mt. Vesuvius in the year 79.

Was a Roman warrior simply showing off his talent when he created this sketch in red chalk on the wall of his barracks in Pompeii, or was he poking fun at military conscription?

Much of these Pompeiian graffiti (an Italian word for "scratching"), in red and white chalk, were clearly legible for many years. This one, obviously the beginning of a far more advanced drawing, was found on the outside wall of a private house, clearly the work of a professional artist. Many political cartoonists of today, and artists in general, begin a drawing by sketching it out this way.

More examples of Roman cartoon and caricature, showing a continuation of the affinity between animals and the "higher order."

From antique amethysts, a lion driving a couple of chickens and a grasshopper driving a pigeon.

Dwarfs and deformed people are, fortunately, no longer considered suitable subjects for the public amusement, and only the imagination of its creator enabled this picture to "live." Pliny insisted that pygmies "mounted upon rams and goats, and armed with bows and arrows . . . . descend in a body during the springtime to the edge of the waters, where they eat the eggs and the young of those birds, not returning to the mountains for three months."

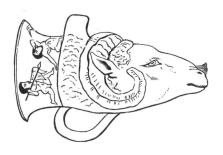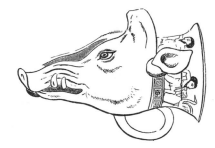

THE MIDDLE AGES

During the Middle Ages, cartoons and caricatures often dealt with such subjects as Death and the Devil, as evidenced in prayerbooks and places of worship, presumably aimed at helping keep a congregation in line, rather than in stitches. Professional craftsmen roamed Europe, incidentally, seeking this kind of work.

From a mass-book of the fourteenth century.

DEVILS SEIZING THEIR PREY. (Bas-relief on the Portal of a Church at Troyes.)

LOST SOULS CAST INTO HELL. (From Queen Mary's Psalter.)

Death and the old man. What more natural way to portray the Grim Reaper than as a bag of bones?

Of course, these cartoonists and caricaturists were pandering to the most backward notions of the wicked and superstitious, but in that they brought with them skilled drawing and a high grade of satire, we can be grateful. However, Emma Phipson attested in her 1896 book, *Choir Stalls and Their Engravings*, (B.T. Batsford, London) that very few people could be blamed for failing to observe this work, because the seats on which most of it appears "were placed so low that it is necessary to crouch on the floor to see them."

The outstretched hands of the Saviour seem well-drawn and able to lend succor to the poor and needy, but some of our ancestors may have wondered what kind of blasphemous cartoonist caused a head to droop that way!

THE 17th TO THE 19th CENTURY

The sailing of the tiny craft Mayflower across the seas, the American and French Revolution, and the U.S. Civil War, all heralded the birth and spread of freedom both in Europe and the New World and kindled similar dreams elsewhere. These three centuries witnessed the emergence of cartoonists who dared to attack corruption, arbitrary actions, or wrong-doings in seats of power heretofore considered immune to criticism. None was spared—church, state, merchant, king, or president—if their actions deserved criticism outraged cartoonists appeared with an accusing brush or pen. In this first group of "Old Masters" are Hogarth, Franklin, Gilray, the Cruikshanks, Leech, Daumier, Nast, Keppler, Davenport, and others. Also included are some cartoons not attributed to a particular artist and a few cartoons by unknown artists. The pages that follow comprise but a sampler of the works produced during these three centuries.

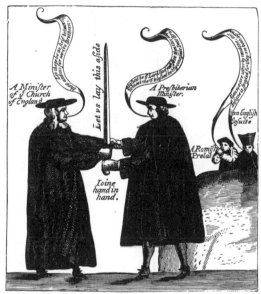

    This drawing, urging a union of the Church of England and the Church of Scotland, used lettering to identify characters and "balloons" to contain the words they were saying, a fore-runner of such technique.

A caricature of the anti-Puritan Prince Rupert drawn by an artist who obviously favored Cromwell.

A comment on the abortive attempt of Charles II to unite the Scots under his rule and with their aid to gain the throne of England.

Another cartoon from the Puritan period, showing the use of lettering to augment a "message." This one is a criticism of tippling in a certain part of Massachusetts.

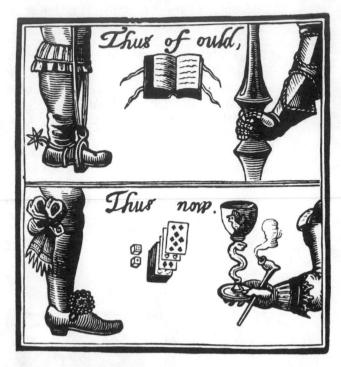

A Puritan and anti-Catholic cartoonist's warning to James II's queen that "It is a foolish sheep that makes the wolf her confessor."

French caricature of corpulent General Galas, who defeated a French Convoy in 1635. The caricature, we may assume, rendered the general speechless. There are no words contained in that balloon.

A Dutch caricature satirizes the collapse of the John Law's Louisiana land-speculation scheme.

"SHARES! SHARES! SHARES!"
The Night Share-crier and his Magic Lantern. A Caricature of John Law and his Bubble Schemes. (Amsterdam, 1720.)

William Hogarth (1697-1764), the celebrated English painter, and considered by many one of its greatest, began his career as a social and political caricaturist. This phase of his work stems directly from the time when young Hogarth's talent for drawing was recognized by his schoolmaster father who apprenticed him to a silver engraver. Hogarth did not stay long as an apprentice but soon opened his own engraving shop. Many of his caricatures originate from this period of his life.

Hogarth does not make it clear whether he is satirizing a dull sermon or an indifferent congregation forced to attend church by the social and religious pressures of the time.

THE SLEEPING CONGREGATION.

As Statues moulder into Worth

TIME SMOKING A PICTURE.

Here Hogarth vents his scorn and bitterness on the contemporary British art dealers who manufacture "old masters."

THE AMERICAN REVOLUTION

Benjamin Franklin (1706-1790), is undoubtedly the father of American political cartooning. At the outbreak of the French and Indian War, the celebrated printer, publisher, author, editor, humorist, inventor, publisher, politician, diplomat and statesman, conceived this figure of a snake, cut into as many parts as there were colonies, that became familiar to thousands of readers of newspapers and handbills.

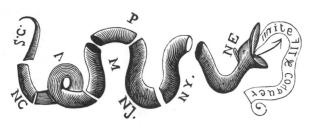

JOIN or DIE

Even if a cut-up snake can't come back to life, Franklin's cartoon did, reappearing in 1765 at the time of the Stamp Act, and again in 1776 when the colonies revolted.

A CARICATURE DESIGNED BY BENJAMIN FRANKLIN.   (London, 1774.)

Explanation by Dr. Franklin: "The Colonies (that is, Britannia's limbs) being severed from her, Britannia is seen lifting her eyes and mangled stumps to heaven; her shield, which she is unable to wield, lies useless by her side; her lance has pierced New England; the laurel branch has fallen from the hand of Pennsylvania; the English oak has lost its head, and stands a bare trunk, with a few withered branches; briers and thorns are on the ground beneath it; the British ships have brooms at their topmast heads, denoting their being on sale; and Britannia herself is seen sliding off the world (no longer able to hold its balance), her fragments overspread with the label, Date obolum Bellisario" (Give a farthing to Belisarius).

Here is another political cartoon that stemmed directly from this most versatile of Americans.

As we can see, the good doctor did not minimize the importance of lettering in a picture, nor was he a slouch at composition.

The seeds of the American Revolution were sown years before the actual occurrence in 1776. Below are two cartoons published in London which convey some idea of the awakening of political sentiment against British arbitrary rule.

THE GOUTY COLOSSUS, WILLIAM PITT (LORD CHATHAM), WITH ONE LEG IN LONDON AND THE OTHER IN NEW YORK. (London, 1766.)

A political protest against England's "ascendancy over the nations of the earth similar to that which Rome had once enjoyed."

THE WIRE-MASTER (BUTE) AND HIS PUPPETS. (London, 1767.)

"The power behind the throne greater than the throne itself."

The criticism was certainly well-founded here. The caricaturist easily could have made Lord Bute a lot more savage and filthy-looking had he chosen to do so.

The French Revolution produced its own crop of domestic and foreign political cartoons favorable and unfavorable to both sides of the conflict.

ASSEMBLY OF THE NOTABLES AT PARIS, FEBRUARY 22D, 1787.*

"Dear objects of my care, I have assembled you to ascertain with what sauce you want to be eaten."
"But we don't want to be eaten at all."
"You are departing from the question."

This vegetarian ape was only speaking for a carnivorous ruling class, the cartoonist might have explained to his editor, regarding the above.

RARE ANIMALS; OR, THE TRANSFER OF THE ROYAL FAMILY FROM THE TUILERIES TO THE TEMPLE.

Above, the caricaturist has spared the livestock, perhaps fearful that he might yet go to the guillotine himself.

THE ESTATES. (Paris, 1789.)

Another cartoon of the period of the French Revolution, showing a very elegant carriage being drawn by a pair of doves. The cartoon, one of a series, attempts to convey the notion that "brotherly love" now again prevails in France because the "third estate" ostensibly has achieved its goals. The third estate, of course, is the road upon which everything moves as before.

There was nothing elegant about this French cartoon, perhaps a kind Ben Franklin abhorred. It is done with the full fury of social and revolutionary upheaval, yet showing plenty of care in execution—of the drawing, that is.

THE NEW CALVARY. (Paris, 1792.)

Louis XVI. crucified by the rebels ; Monsieur and the Comte d'A
bound by the decrees of the factions ; Robespierre, mounted upon
Constitution, presents the sponge soaked in regicides' gall ; the Q
overwhelmed with grief, demands speedy vengeance ;

It is interesting to note that in this period of stress, some artists did not allow their emotions to run away with them. Both these drawings are done in a "tight," or careful style.

THE ZENITH OF FRENCH GLORY—A VIEW IN PERSPECTIVE.

In this remarkable cartoon, we see that the "savagery" ascribed to James Gillray is truly contained in his work. Still, there might hardly have been reason to cast aspersions on his ancestors, for who can tell if the artist condoned or condemned the gory spectacle he portrayed so well here?

Napoleon and his period proved to be a source of brilliant cartoons for the contemporary caricaturists.

A GREAT MAN'S LAST LEAP—NAPOLEON GOING ON BOARD THE EN-GLISH FRIGATE, ASSISTED BY THE FAITHFUL BERTRAND. (Paris, 1815.)

Here is the "Little Colonel" as he nimbly changes ships in midstream.

This caricature is attributed to the famous French painter Delacroix, who almost provided a balloon for each head.

TALLEYRAND—THE MAN WITH SIX HEADS. (Paris, 1817.)

The post-Revolutionary period in America of course did not bring an end to the activities of the political cartoonists despite the conclusion of the war with Britain. Now the domestic problems of the new nation occupied the minds, brushes, and pens of the cartoonists. Below are two examples.

FIGHT IN CONGRESS BETWEEN LYON AND GRISWOLD, FEBRUARY 15TH, 1798.

"He in a trice struck Griswold thrice
Upon his head, enraged, sir;
Who seized the tongs to ease his wrongs,
And Griswold thus engaged, sir."

A couple of politicos forsake oratory in favor of another, less gentle form of persuasion, providing good action drawing, courtesy of both beligerents and nearly all those present. In those days, some political cartoonists believed the busier a picture, the better.

THE GERRY-MANDER. (Boston, 1811.)

The famous Gerrymander by Gilbert Stuart caricatured the redistricting of Essex County, Massachusetts by Democratic-Republican Party leaders in 1811 in order to insure the election of two members of the party to the Senate. The salamander-like cartoon was named for Governor Elbridge Gerry who although opposed to the measure signed the redistricting bill.

James Gillray (1757-1815), is considered by many to be the finest British satiric artist of all time. Draper Hill, in his biography *Mr. Gillray, the Caricaturist*, (Phaidon Press, London) says; "More than any other, this solitary, second-generation Scot lifted his calling from a trade into an art."

In the beginning, Gillray's inspiration and idol was the famous master Hogarth. However, on the advice of friends, he began concentrating on political affairs, and soon realized he had found his niche.

Coming into his own during an era, when conservatism ruled the arts, Gillray often portrayed the leading personalities of the day in brutal

caricature, to the consternation of many—including King George III—who had hitherto only seen themselves through the eyes of Sir Joshua Reynolds and other "pretty" painters.

In 1802, Gillray issued a set of four plates entitled "The Consequences of a Successful French Landing," in which he depicted the horrors of Napoleon's threatened invasion of England. These plates were credited with a revival of patriotism that ultimately made the Emperor's aggrandizement impossible.

Hailed by critics, Gillray's prints were collected feverishly right within his own lifetime, many of them being snatched up the instant they appeared in his publisher's shop, a scant few hundred yards from St. James's Palace. Newspapers of the day stated that the buying excitement

he KING of BROBDINGNAG and GULLIVER

was indescribable. Inevitably, as Gillray's fame spread, his influence was felt professionally on both sides of the Atlantic. According to Draper Hill, a German journalist in 1806 introduced the caricaturist to his readers as the "foremost living artist in the whole of Europe."

Hill, the editorial cartoonist of the *Commercial Appeal*, concludes: "Gillray was in the highest sense a professional. It was his lot to serve as jester to the *beau monde*, surrounded by aristocrats and would-be aristocrats, obliged to work up the inspirations of dilettante amateurs. He was scarcely less of a foreigner in St. James's Street than Marco Polo at the court of Kublai Khan. Every honest critic must be in some respect an outsider; Gillray's remarkable vision was conditioned by his temperamental and social detachment from his environment. He poured himself into his work, an art so wedded to the moment that nine years after he died an editor could complain that much of it had become unintelligible for want of explanation."

THE KING OF BROBDINGNAG AND GULLIVER.

TALLEYRAND, KING-AT-ARMS, BEARING HIS MASTER'S
GENEALOGICAL TREE, SPRINGING FROM BUONE, BUTCHER.

NAPOLEON IN HIS CORONATION ROBES.

FIGURES FROM GILLRAY'S NAPOLEONIC CARICATURES.

(Each of these is invaluable to students of political cartooning, for its depth and penetration.)

Robert Cruikshank (1789-1856), the son of the caricaturist Isaac Cruikshank, together with his brother George influenced generations of British cartoonists. In this tongue-in-cheek joke, Robert Cruikshank shows John Bull's feet securely fastened in stocks, the weight of the last war's taxes on his head, so he is hardly in a position to help Spain even if he wanted to. The King of France looks on from his mount on a cannon pulled by the Pope, Russia, Austria, and Prussia."

R. CRUIKSHANK   *Published, May,* 1823.

"JOHN BULL FLOURISHING IN A DIGNIFIED ATTITUDE OF STRICT NEUTRALITY !!!!"

HOPE—A PHRENOLOGICAL ILLUSTRATION. (George Cruikshank, 1826.)

John Leech (1817-1864), was another British cartoonist and caricaturist, who could spoof Mother England, although she was still mourning the loss of her American colonies. Leech, the son of an Irishman, from whom he inherited his artistic bent, was born in London and educated at Charterhouse a famous "public" (i.e. private) school for boys; William Thackeray the future novelist-artist was one of his classmates. At 16, Leech began to study medicine, but the chance selling of some sketches of London street characters caused him to change professions abruptly.

The Landing of William the Conqueror.

Madame de Montfort astonishing the French fleet.

At first, Leech dealt in social subjects, doing lithograph illustrations for Dickens' *A Christmas Carol* in 1844, and *A Comic History of Rome* in 1852, the latter in woodcuts. He worked closely with George Cruikshank on other projects, and for a while their work bore remarkable similarity.

Becoming more and more political, Leech soon developed the style that was uniquely his own, a technique for which he became most famous and the one with which he is most frequently associated: etchings printed in color. Leech's association with *Punch* began in 1844 and, lasting until his death, brought forth some of his greatest works.

Edward II. resigning his Crown.

The Bishop of Ely presenting a pottle of Strawberries to the Duke of Glo'ster.

From John Leech, aspiring political cartoonists may learn that the best satire is attained only by the best drawing. Careless exaggeration is not the answer. In all Leech's work, there is beauty and realism. We accept it because it is the *truth*.

The close resemblance of Leech's work to George Cruikshank's can be assessed in this drawing by the latter. Such "coincidence" is common among young cartoonists and caricaturists, but they usually develop styles of their own and go their separate ways.

Term Time. (George Cruikshank, 1827.)

An amusing caricature by John Leech gently poking fun at George I. This is one of 220 woodcuts and colored etchings Leech drew for *The Comic History of England*.

Honoré Daumier (1808-1874) was born in Marseilles, the son of a glazier. He was taken to Paris at the age of seven because his parents thought Honoré would have a better opportunity for success in the capital. Fortunately, in the beginning, the boy did only fairy well at such odd jobs as messenger in a law court and clerking in a book store.

Requesting that he be given a chance to study drawing, Daumier's parents reluctantly yielded and he was apprenticed to one Alexandre Lenoir, an academician who could do little to hold his pupil's interest. Young Daumier preferred to wander about the streets of Paris, examining the people and the slums in which they lived. It is easy to assume that he must have also pondered the causes of such poverty while making numerous sketches and spending time visiting the Louvre. Anyway, in 1828 Daumier became a student at the Paris Academy and began drawing illustrations for popular magazines. Two years later, resenting the injustices of the monarchy, he made his first political cartoons.

Notice the contrast in feeling the artist has given the figure on the table, and those about to dismember it.

THE CONSTITUTION ON THE DISECTING TABLE

The hatred of Daumier for the ruling class is clearly shown in this gluttonous character enjoying the view from his balcony.

THE ROYAL PEACE AND ORDER

Cold and deadly, these fine, feathered friends, not at all the kind of birds the American naturalist Audubon would select for a water color.

THE WAR STRATEGISTS

Hardpressed for money and the material things of life, Daumier tried for a while to produce academic pictures that might readily sell, usually finding subjects he liked in such places as second-class railway compartments. But an inborn sympathy for the people he drew or painted, coupled with his natural contempt for social injustice, could not keep the biting satire out of his work. The advent of the July Revolution (1830), which aroused thousands of citizens eager for a rebirth of freedom, stirred Daumier, who had not yet truly been able to express himself professionally. He joined the staff of the weekly magazine *Silhouette*, then later in 1831, *La Caricature*, where the only requirements of an artist were that he have "indignation at heart and a verve at the end of his crayon."

The warmth and beauty of peace, balanced precariously on a cold, iron cannon—a perfect cartoon concept, masterfully executed.

THE BED OF PEACE

Daumier fitted in perfectly at *La Caricature*, doing many lithographs dedicated to the cause of political freedom and the cessation of repressive measures. In fact, one picture of his displayed in the window of the publication, entitled "Gargantua" and obviously referring to King Louis Philippe, aroused such passions in its viewers that a demonstration resulted and both Daumier and his publisher were seized and imprisoned for six months. However, incarceration failed to dampen Daumier's spirits. He emerged from a cell more fiery than ever, commencing his famous series of busts which portrayed how he thought of all the noted jurists and politicians of France. In subsequent lithographs (and there would be almost 4,000 plates before blindness halted him) he never hesitated to search for truth by showing the cruel monstrosities taking place under the guise of justice. Yet, amazingly, he also was able to produce any number of classical paintings that received the highest critical acclaim.

PEACE IDYLL

To Daumier, the beauty of woman symbolized the beauty of life. Had he not drawn them so well, his countrymen might not have been so deeply moved by his work!

FROM RIGHT AND LEFT THEY TUG ON THE REPUBLIC—THUS PRODUCING A BALANCE

Here Daumier satirizes hypocritical peace makers. The slashing attack is absent but the message, despite the gentle sculptor and the handsome statue, comes across: hypocracy is exposed.

A NEW PROPOSITION FOR A STATUE OF PEACE

But a political cartoonist must also be able to draw the bad and the ugly, as Daumier shows here.

DISARMAMENT—"AFTER YOU"

ALL OF MOTHER DIPLOMACY'S LULLABIES DON'T HELP— LITTLE MARS WILL NOT SLEEP

ROBERT MACAIRE FISHING FOR SHARE-HOLDERS.

This drawing by Daumier was done as part of a series attacking the French government, in collusion with Charles Philipon, the publisher of *Charivari*, who provided the "gags." Using outside ideas is common practice with some cartoonists who find drawing time-consuming enough, although in Daumier's case such a practice was exceptional.

Fifty million Frenchmen (or whatever the population was then) shared Honoré Daumier's emotions, give or take a few aristocrats.

THE FUTURE—THE MASKED WRESTLER

GALILEO WONDERS ABOUT THE TRANSFORMATION OF THE EARTH'S CRUST

THE NEW CINDERELLA

THE RUSSIAN BEAR, THE MOST DANGEROUS OF ALL BEAR

THE NEW WORLD

Back in the New World, no sign of a Daumier had yet appeared on the artistic horizon, but there were drawings dealing with the foibles of the rich, the less than rich, and even the poor, most of them neatly done, if not with any particular depth or perspicacity.

N. B.

These Young Gentlemen are not indulging in the Filthy Habit of Smoking. They are only Chewing Toothpicks, the comforting and elegant Practice now so much in Vogue.

THE GREAT TOBACCO CONTROVERSY.

CLARA (*emphatically*). "I don't care what you say, Frank—I shall always think it a *nasty, odious, dirty, filthy, disgusting*, and *most objectionable* Habit!"

FRANK. "Haw!—Now I'm really surprised, Clara, to hear such a Clever Girl as you are running down Smoking in such Strong Language—for it's admitted by all Sensible People, you know, that it's the *Abuse of Tobacco* that's Wrong!"

[*Which little bit of sophistry completely vanquished Clara.*

THE PRESENT STYLE OF BEARD—TWO SAMPLES.

Thus, cartoonists were on the job, giving the people a look at themselves with more jokes, one-liners, two-liners, and sometimes no lines at all.

BEFORE THE PANIC
Little Girl to Dry Goods Merchant. "Please, Sir, may I—" Merchant. "No. no: go away, go away, there, little girl! You oughtn't to come in here."

AFTER THE PANIC
Same Merchant To Same Little Girl. "Three Cents' worth Thread? Yes, my little Dear, directly.
Any thing more? and how's your mamma?

A MORAL LESSON FROM THE NURSERY.

ARTHUR. "Do you know, Freddy, that we are only made of Dust!"
FREDDY. "Are we?   Then I'm sure we ought to be very careful how we pitch
into each other so, for fear we might crumble each other all to pieces!"

A HINT TO DRY GOODS MEN.
The handsome Clerk always attracts the Ladies.

THE SPIRITUALIST.   THE MATERIALIST.

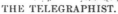

THE TELEGRAPHIST.   THE NATURALIST.

There was only one trouble, sometimes in the new, growing society certain jokes couldn't be regarded as funny by *everybody*. The black people of America, for instance, were receiving their greatest insults and degradation. But who was there to speak up for them, to draw them with honor?

The U.S. Civil War. The Union, banded together under one flag since achieving independence from King George, suddenly trembled on the brink of civil war and it was time for men with pen and ink, and just about everybody else, to take sides.

MISTRESS COLUMBIA, WHO HAS BEEN TAKING A NAP, SUDDENLY WAKES UP AND CALLS HER NOISY SCHOLARS TO ORDER.

The lady, also known as "Gem of the Ocean," is here pictured as a schoolmarm very much displeased with her rowdy, boisterous class on both sides of that Mason-Dixon line clearly drawn down the center of the little old schoolhouse. An amusing cartoon, pertinent to the fateful history about to unfold.

In this cartoon, *Harper's Weekly*, which had been founded originally to promote the firm's books, was still trying to be fair to both sides editorially, but as we can see by one of the slaves shown here, the blacks were getting nothing out of the detente except maybe tired.

THE NORTH AND THE SOUTH.

SOUTH. "Don't you dar to talk to me, Sir!"
NORTH. "Oh! yeou be derned!"

NORTH. "Lookee here, South, I'm gittin' rayther cold."
SOUTH. "Well, North, can't say I'm cold, but am bloody hungry. Now—you want my Cotton."
NORTH. "No dern yeou, you want my Corn! Yeou—acknowledge the Cor—."
SOUTH. "No; you Cotton to me."—They Compromise!

The Compromise (Selection First and Last.—"The North, in consideration of the fact that the South Acknowledges The Corn, do hereby agree to Cotton To The South."

Glorious, magnificent, and triumphant effect of the Compromise. The Constitution and the Nigger to be supported. Our Ramparts to be built of Cotton and Corn. Hurrah-h-h-h!

THE AMERICAN EAGLE SURPRISES JEFF DAVIS IN HIS ATTEMPT TO
ROB HER NEST.

"War is a continuation of politics," said a Prussian general, and cartoonists on both sides of the Mason-Dixon line took different views of the
Civil War. Here was the viewpoint of ones from the North.

Two excellent animal drawings, from the Union point of view—the fox
properly villainous, and the goose—well, just a silly goose.

That Sly Fox, Jeff, trying to induce Miss-
Souri (silly goose) to take a walk in the woods
of Secession, and

What the Result would be.

A cartoon showing an army that could indeed travel on its stomach.

REINFORCEMENTS FOR OUR VOLUNTEERS ON THE MARCH SOUTHWARD.

UNCLE SAM. "Hallo there, you Rascal! where are you going with my Property, eh?"
JEFF. DAVIS. "Oh, dear Uncle! ALL I WANT IS TO BE LET ALONE."

Notice how handsome and forthright Uncle Sam appears though entirely subdued in shadows, and how dark and villainous Jefferson Davis appears even in the light.

LINCOLN AND THE NEGRO QUESTION—A GERMAN CARTOON
NEGRO: "May I be so bold—"
LINCOLN: "Step nearer, my friend."
SOUTHERN STATESMAN: "Then I beg to be excused." (He secedes from the Union.)

Another cartoon sympathetic to the North.

M'Clellan.   Barlow.   Belmont.
"ON TO RICHMOND!"—THE PENINSULAR CAMPAIGN. (1862.)

M'Clellan. "You must coax him along: conciliate him. Force won't do. I don't believe in it; but don't let go. Keep his head to the rear. If he should get away, he might go to Richmond, and then my plans for conquering the Rebellion will never be developed."

B–lm–t. "Hold fast, B–rl–w, or he *will* get to Richmond in spite of us; and then my capital for the European market is all lost."

B–rl–w. "I've got him fast; there's no danger. He's only changing his base to the Gun-boats."

B–lm–t. "Look out for that letter to the President which you wrote for him. Don't lose that."

As we can see above, the "Democratic" mule was already up for grabs as a symbol by any interested parties.

The war from the point of view of the Confederacy, as seen by various political cartoonists.

VIRGINIA PAUSING.

Note that the Great Emancipator is merely a great big pussycat here!

JOHN BULL--IED!

ABRAHAM LINCOLN—(with unparalelled ferocity)—See here—naow—you Johnie, jes' stop them Rebel Rams, or I'll *lamb* you!

LITTLE JOHNNIE RUSSELL.—Don't be impatient, Mr. Lincoln, I'm just about to paint my broad arrow on them—meanwhile, you see that little Invoice of Arms you ordered is ready for shipment.

In every war, the enemy grows uglier and one's own side better looking. Northern sympathizers, in this case, would hardly recognize Lincoln here, though indeed they knew he was no Beau Brummell.

MASKS AND FACES.

King Abraham before and after issuing the EMANCIPATION PROCLAMATION.

Up North, they called him Honest Abe—

—down South he was known to be two-faced, with at least one of them devilish.

THE YANKEE CAVALRY SENT TO INTERCEPT GEN. STUART.

A great joke—on both sides, perhaps—the poor slaves who could even be the subject of a bad pun!

THE YANKEE SOLDIERS' NIGHTMARE.

A VISION OF THE BLACK-HORSE CAVALRY!!!

"I WISH I WAS IN DIXIE!"

Plaintive Air—Sung nightly in Washington by that Celebrated Delineator, Abraham Lincoln.

A more sympathetic Southern caricature of Abe Lincoln here, showing him almost soulful!

RECONSTRUCTION!

What we may expect under its benign influence.

The greatest Southern incitement of all, a lowly black in the army of occupation, and as if that weren't enough, another black amused by such a spectacle!

An extremely boyish-looking President castigates his generals here, perhaps to make immaturity seem another of his vices.

HOOLMASTER LINCOLN AND HIS BOYS.—*Lincoln*—Waal, boys, what's the matter with yer; you haint been hurt, hev yer ? *McClellan.*—Them rs that run away has been beatin' us. *Lincoln.*—What fellers ? *McClellan.*—Bob Lee and Jeb Stuart and them. *Lincoln.*—I sent you out to s them came fellers back, so's I could wallop 'em. *McClellan.*—Yes, but Bob Lee took and bunged me in the eye. *Pope*—And Stunwall son he kicked me in the rear until he broke my arm. *Banks.*—Yes, and that same feller gouged me and rus me until I run my leg off and to wear a wooden one. *Burnside.*—All of 'em, Bob Lee, Stunwall and Stuart, jumped on me at Fredericksburg and give me fits ; that's the n my jaw is tied up, to keep my teeth from chatterin', for I've had a fit of the ager ever since. *Lincoln.*—You are a worthless set, all of You haint no spunk. I'm agoin' to spank every one of yer. Come up here.

A very fine action drawing,—purporting to show the *joie de vivre* of being a dog-catcher.

This colored person is NOT engaged in the capture of conscripts, as will doubtless be asserted by certain Yankee prisoners who witness the operation from the windows of the "Libby," when they return North.

The clouded crystal ball: a political cartoonist of 1861—one friendly to the North, moreover, yet put forth the "amusing" notion that there might be an attempt made on the life of President Lincoln!

The moral of this might be that, even in war, drawings and ideas should have *taste*.

THE FLIGHT OF ABRAHAM.
(As Reported by a Modern Daily Paper.)

(1) THE ALARM

"On Thursday night, after he had retired, Mr. Lincoln was aroused, and informed that a stranger desired to see him on a matter of life and death. ***A conversation elicited the fact that an organized body of men had determined that Mr. Lincoln should never leave the City of Baltimore alive. ***Statesmen laid the plan, Bankers indorsed it, and Adventurers were to carry it into effect."

(2) THE COUNCIL

"Mr. Lincoln did not want to yield, and his friends cried with indignation. But they insisted, and he left."

(3) THE SPECIAL TRAIN

"He wore a Scotch plaid Cap and a very long Military Cloak, so that he was entirely unrecognizable."

(4) THE OLD COMPLAINT

"Mr. Lincoln, accompanied by Mr. Seward, paid his respects to President Buchanan, spending a few minutes in general conversation."

Across the ocean, Sir John Tenniel (1820-1914) illustrator of Lewis Carroll's *Alice in Wonderland* reflected in this cartoon on how the South might view Lincoln's issuance of the Emancipation Proclamation.

SCENE FROM THE AMERICAN "TEMPEST"
Caliban (Sambo): "You beat him 'nough, Massa! Berry little time I'll beat him, too."

Thomas Nast (1840-1902), born in Germany and taken to the United States when he was six years old, was destined to become the greatest political cartoonist of the Civil War, and probably in all American history for that matter. He studied at the National Academy of Design and grew up admiring Leech and Tenniel, among others. At 15, his first drawing was accepted by Frank Leslie's *Illustrated Newspaper*. He went to Europe several years later to cover a boxing match and Garibaldi's Italian campaign freeing Sicily and Naples. Barely 20 when Fort Sumter was fired upon and the secession of states took place, he turned into a fiery Union patriot. *Harper's Weekly,* strongly pro-North by this time, was quick to welcome him to its pages.

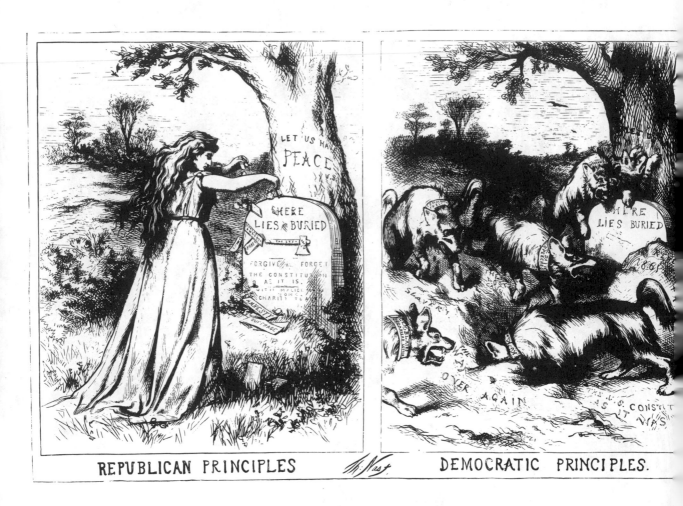

Nast's Republican sympathies did not subside with the end of the Civil War as this cartoon shows.

A TRUCE—NOT A COMPROMISE, BUT A CHANCE FOR HIGH-TONED GENTLEMEN TO RETIRE GRACEFULLY FROM THEIR VERY CIVIL DECLARATIONS OF WAR.

Again we see that Nast has not let up on the Democrats in this powerful cartoon in which he charges the Tilden supporters with threatening another civil war unless their candidate is declared the victor in the Hayes-Tilden Presidential contest.

"Nast's efforts on behalf of the North, were not confined to the usual black-and-white cartoons. The tempera painting, on the next page, was one of a number he exhibited in New York and Boston under the title "Grand Caricaturama." Of it, Lloyd Goodrich, advisory director of the Whitney Museum of Modern Art, says:

In explanation of the symbolism in this scene, a newspaper review of the Boston exhibition said that Columbia, after landing on Plymouth Rock and being greeted by the genius of Liberty, 'soon becomes acquainted with Jonathan, marries him, and they set up housekeeping. She is shocked to find he has slaves, and the picture which represents them at home is very funny. She is looking sorrowfully at a crowd of the most comical little darkies, while Jonathan, with hands thrust in his pockets, and evidently whistling to himself, is gazing at the statues with which some 'prophetic artist' has decorated his hall.'"

The over-lifesize statues include some of Nast's pet hates, including two fellow-journalists. The press in these violently partisan days carried on intra-professional vendettas that would have brought libel action today. Democratic and Republican papers exchanged insults, editors pilloried their opposite numbers, even caricaturists caricatured each other. To Nast, anything Democratic was "Copperhead," and called for the corresponding symbol.

From left to right: Manton Marble, editor of *The World*, (who later prostituted his paper to the Tweed Ring), as Atlas bowed beneath the globe, which is encircled by a copperhead. Next toward the right, as "Gladiator," the Honorable John Morrissey, ex-pugilist, immigrant runner, barroom and gambling-house proprietor, a power in Tammany Hall, elected to Congress the preceding year, later a state senator. Then Andrew Johnson as Moses holding a tablet inscribed "Veto." (Among his injudicious public statements, Johnson had told the Negroes, "I am your Moses.") In the background, as the Devil, Fernando Wood, adroit and corrupt Mayor of New York (1854 to 1861), proslavery if it suited his purposes; when the Southern states were about to secede from the Union, he had officially suggested that New York City secede with them. Nast had published an identical caricature of him in *Harper's Weekly*. Finally, at the right, James Gordon Bennett, Sr., founder and editor of the New York *Herald*, brilliant and cynical journalist, as Apollo with a lyre—undoubtedly a pun.

It is noteworthy that the Negroes are the liveliest element in the painting, contrasting with the cold marmoreal statues—or, for that matter, with Columbia and Jonathan. Certainly there is mockery in the father's low bow and the children's antics in front of the statues.

Nast's wife was said to have served as his model for "Columbia" and, presumably, whenever the figure of an attractive lady was needed in his pictures.

Here is Thomas Nast on the subject of minorities.

The cartoonist's lady has indignation written all over her face, enough of it to show how Nast himself probably felt about racial "superiority."

THE CHINESE QUESTION.—

COLUMBIA.—"HANDS OFF, GENTLEMEN! AMERICA MEANS FAIR PLAY FOR ALL MEN."

Nast symbolizes the "uprisings" by the Sioux and other tribes in the years after the Civil War, in this cartoon of an Indian standing his ground despite the menace of a nineteenth-century "minion of the law."

"MOVE ON!"

HAS THE NATIVE AMERICAN NO RIGHTS THAT THE NATURALIZED AMERICAN IS BOUND TO RESPECT?

The war between the states ended at Appomattox Courthouse, Virginia, in 1865, but the fighting continued on other fronts for Thomas Nast.

Church and State—No Union Upon Any Terms.

The "Third Term" Trap
U.S.G. "If that don't fetch the animal, Governor, don't blame me any more."

Outstanding among these was the battle he waged in New York against Boss Tweed and the Tammany Ring who were plundering the city ruthlessly.

What was this Tammany that it became such a colossus of corruption, one of the most hated institutions in American politics? Organized as a private club on Manhattan Island in 1789, by early members of the Democratic Party, it was dedicated to "the independence, the popular liberty and the federal union of the Country, and whatever may perpetuate the love of freedom. . ." The name had come from a legendary chief of the Delaware Indians. The club headquarters, where gathered all the powerful party forces, came to be known as "the wigwam." Wigwams were established all over the country, but the center of action remained in New York's Manhattan.

It is true that Tammany began as a fraternal order, with liberal interests, helping promote jobs for thousands of immigrants. It supported legislation such as workingmen's suffrage and the abolition of debtors' prison, and later backed the New Deal programs of Franklin Delano Roosevelt, with its social security and unemployment insurance. Nevertheless, it is the flagrant dishonesty of the party "bosses" for which Tammany is best remembered.

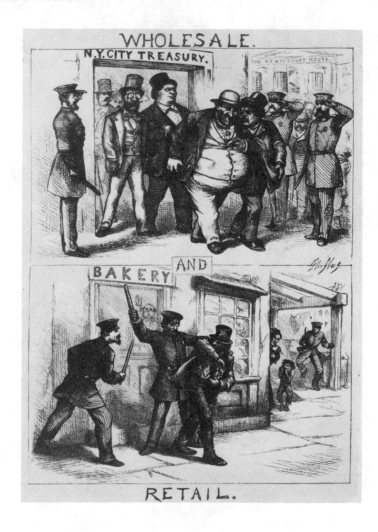

William Marcy Tweed was one of these bosses, inheriting a mantle formerly worn by none other than Aaron Burr, who had even made money supplying drinking water to the people of New York through a company in which he was a principal stockholder.

Three symbols "invented" by Thomas Nast. He was also responsible for another, the figure of Santa Claus, as that jolly old gent is known throughout parts of the civilized world.

Tweed, who came to power in Tammany Hall in 1857, had started his career in the volunteer fire department—apparently there was an easy dollar to be made if people *really* wanted a blaze put out. Rubbing shoulders with Democratic ward heelers, he had become a member of "The Forty Thieves" of one of the wards, then stepped into Congress, where he

TWEEDLEDEE AND SWEEDLEDUM.
(*A New Christmas Pantomime at Tammany Hall.*)
Clown (to Pantaloon). " Let's blind them with *this*, and then take *some more.*"
TWEED'S GIFT OF FIFTY THOUSAND DOLLARS TO THE POOR OF HIS NATIVE WARD.

distinguished himself by acquiring avoirdupois rather than a grasp of the issues of the day.

In spite of a slight deficiency in academics, Tweed wangled an appointment to the New York City school commission, The pay was insignificant, but Tweed was able to compensate for this by selling textbooks to the city (fraudulently), and also by extorting money from teachers who wished to secure positions within the school system. In another job to which Tweed helped himself, he was even able to determine which ferry boat lines could ply the waters of the East River between Manhattan and Brooklyn!

"I don't care what they print about me, most of my constituents can't read anyway—but them damn pictures!"

These were the famous words of Tweed before his arrest and subsequent conviction as a direct result of Thomas Nast's campaign against him.

THE BRAIN

Chicken feed. Tweed soon became supreme in New York's Democratic Party as a state senator and chairman of Tammany's Executive Committee. Indeed, he was now *"Boss"* Tweed.

This, then, was the man that Thomas Nast made the subject of his great series of cartoons in *Harper's Weekly*. And it was during this period that Tweed tried to buy the silence of *The New York Times* with a bribe of

$5,000,000 to its owner, and offering a substantial amount to Nast too, "so he could go abroad and study art."

Both offers were rejected. The *Times's* editorials continued, as did Nast's cartoons. The sum total of their accusations: *the people of New York City had already been bilked of over $200,000,000!*

Tweed ordered all Harper-printed textbooks banned in New York City classrooms. He tried to buy a majority of stock in the *Times*. His efforts were in vain. Reformers mobilized, demanding the ouster of Boss Tweed and the smashing of his "Ring." He was brought to trial and found guilty on 104 counts, and sentenced to 12 years in prison—where his occupation was listed as "statesman."

"WHO STOLE THE PEOPLE'S MONEY?" — DO TELL . N.Y.TIMES.   'TWAS HIM

Released shortly later, through legal maneuvering, Tweed fled the country while awaiting trial on new charges, but was brought back from Spain where someone had recognized him from a Thomas Nast cartoon! He died in jail, a pauper.

Nast on other subjects:

What We Must Do About It.
Citizen Hercules, make a clean sweep of the dirt and the cause.

Another Nast cartoon in defense of minorities, the graffiti on the wall again telling us his loathing of bigotry.

"Every Dog," (No Distinction of Color) "Has His Day."
Red Gentleman to Yellow Gentleman. Pale face 'fraid
you crowd him out, as he did me."

Unpredictable politically, Nast might be accused of conservatism in this illustration for an editorial describing the movement for an eight-hour day as "mainly led by foreigners who scarcely speak our language and who have no knowledge of the country nor comprehension of American institutions."

Too Heavy A Load For The Trades-Unions.
The competent workman must support the incomp

A cartoon on a "local" issue, the disgraceful condition of city streets, as far as sanitation was concerned. "New York was able to deal with Tweed, and it is quite able to deal with Tweed tactics," stated *Harper's Weekly*. But this superb drawing and composition might have made some of its readers, as well as the mayor himself, forget the whole issue of public health, had the situation not been so critical.

The Political Ajax Defying The Gods.

Split the mud and drown him.

Nast never stopped his attacks on the spoils system.

PAN-IC IN SESSION
Death to us (the people) and fun for them ("Statesmen").

Charles Stanley Reinhart (1844-1896) displayed full faith in h
Executive on the occasion of the Spanish Government in Cuba co
"atrocities" against American citizens, via "drumhead court ma
this point in time, the symbol of Cuba naturally became as beau
as Reinhart could draw.

THE CUBAN QUESTION.—*(From a Sketch by Ashton Lunt.)*
President Grant. "Let's be sure we're Right, then go ahead!"

EDITORIAL AND POLITICAL CARTOONING

Joseph Keppler (1838-1894) drew this cartoon for the readers of Frank Leslie's *Illustrated Newspaper*. They had to be just that—*readers*. Indeed, a survey might have shown them spending more time reading the printer's type and hand lettering in this drawing, than in studying the drawing itself. But then, apparently, there was so much story to tell, of graft and corruption and ward heelers and politicians, not to mention dead rats!

THE LATE TERRIBLE DEMOCRATIC STORM.

U.S.G.—"What a sorry plight we are in! See what bad holes the storm has made in the umbrella! Blaine, can't you stop that one?"

James B.—"I am trying my best, but this Bloody Shirt won't do it; I am afraid we are all lost."

Kelley—"Oh, my poor dear baby! It is getting very wet. It won't take much more to kill it."

Tilden—"Ah, my men, 'Honesty is the best policy.' If your umbrella ever was of good firm stuff, it has become too rotten in your hands to protect you against this storm."

"The anti-inflation sentiment and determination of the people to put down 'Bossism' " were responsible for a setback at the polls for the Democrats, according to an editorial in the *Illustrated Newspaper*, and gave Keppler a chance to show readers exactly how to draw a fallen Tammany equestrienne.

THROWN FROM HIS HIGH HORSE; Or, ANOTHER CHECK TO ONE-MAN POWER.
U.S.G.—"Ah, Kelly, I tried to ride that same horse, and you might have been warned by my example. There's no love lost between us, 'tis true, but I can't help condoling with you. Boo-hoo!"

More cartoons by Keppler. Although his work seemed lighter in mood, he succeeded Nast as America's favorite political cartoonist by 1870.

OUT OF THE FOLD.

"Oh, dreadful! They dwell in peace and harmony, and have no church scandals. They must be wiped out."

In this mild spoof of organized religion for *Puck*, of which he was a part owner, Keppler gives us an indication of his former profession of dramatic actor, in the way some of these "bluenoses" are registering horror.

This Keppler rout in "the Congressional barnyard," showing the GOP elephant attempting to make fricassee out of a flock of poultry representatives, without caring where the feathers might fall, probably frightened the gizzards out of some Democrats suspected of *fowl* play.

WHAT IS FUN TO THE ELEPHANT, IS DEATH TO THE CHICKENS.

(detail)

WELCOME TO ALL!

Here is the political cartoonist with his gripes and grievances put aside for the moment, simply proud of his country and reminding one and all that America is a place of refuge for any who wish to make it their home.

To illustrate a big, ugly problem Congress had been sidestepping, Keppler presented it as a big, ugly monster, right on the floor of the House where he thought it belonged.

THE OPENING OF THE CONGRESSIONAL SESSION

Another cartoon poking fun at the people's representatives, showing them rendering Uncle Sam *really* flat broke, maybe flatter than anybody ever imagined possible.

THE U. S. WRINGER.
$150,000,000 Surplus Revenue Wrung from Patient Taxpayers for the Benefit of Jobbers and Monopolists.

Here Kepler warns both parties that the independent voter is likely to be the decisive factor in future elections.

WEIGHED IN THE BALANCE.

Bror Thure Thulstrup (1848-1930), the *Harper's Weekly* cartoonist, needed practically no lettering and only that tiger in a quack doctor's clothing (and pince-nez glasses) to tell readers all they had to know about Democratic Party aspirations in 1880.

"A CHANGE IS NECESSARY,"—Democratic Cry.

Doctor Democracy. "You say that you are prosperous, happy, content, have abundance, are in perfect health, and at peace with everybody, etc.—Hum!—Well, madam, you put your case in *my* hands, and we'll soon CHANGE all that!"

W.A. Rogers (1854-1931) worked for and contributed to many of America's great publications including *Harper's*, *Life*, the *New York Herald*, and the *Washington Post*.

HE WANTS THEM BOTH

W.A. Rogers shows us that despite the great job Nast had done on Boss Tweed, there was still a Tammany Hall!

Here, in another fine drawing, Rogers deals with a powerful chairman of the New York State Republican Committee, Thomas Platt, considered by many to be a worse person to deal with than the new Tammany boss, Richard ("The Squire") Croker.

A Few Pointers From An Expert.
Platts new Sunday-School class.

Homer Davenport (1867-1912) was another cartoonist to take on the Tammany tiger. Davenport, who came from Silverton, Oregon, was formerly employed by the San Francisco *Examiner*. The artist has just caught the tiger in the act of knocking a hat off the head of Richard ("The Squire") Croker. Thanks to Tammany—and to Nast, who gave the club the tiger image—all political cartoonists of the day had to be great cat artists, and here we have an interesting study of one's paw.

  Who, now, was this new "Boss" Croker? He arrived in America with his parents from Ireland as a child in 1846, the year of the potato blight. As a tough gangleader at 19, he attracted the attention of two Tam-

The Revolt Against Bossism.

many stalwarts, Jimmy "The Famous" O'Brien and "Honest John" Kelly. Pushed along by them, Croker occupied public office, first as an alderman, then as coroner. Eventually driven behind the scenes by various scandals, he succeeded Kelly as leader of Tammany, handing out public service franchises, making decisions on city purchases and contracts, and beginning to wield much influence nationally. During the 1890's, Croker or-

The Reward Of Virtue.

ganized the "United Colored Democracy" to attract votes of black citizens that normally went to the party of Lincoln. Croker appointed mayors, judges and governors, and had a hand in winning 17 elections. By the time he stepped down in his mid-60's, his power far exceeded that ever acquired by Boss Tweed. Unlike Tweed, he did not die broke.

That tiger couldn't look vicious all the time, or people like Davenport would have grown bored with their work. There's ample savagery for both on Boss Croker's face here, anyway.

But political cartoonist Davenport, had other targets for his work, for which he had been brought east by publisher William Randolph Hearst. One of these was Marcus Alonzo Hanna, appointed U.S. Senator from Ohio in 1897.

What were Mark Hanna's credentials that inspired political cartoonists to make him their prey? Born in the Buckeye State, he had received his education there and been associated with his father in the wholesale grocery business. Then Hanna went into coal and iron with his wife's side of the family, followed that with investments in shipyards and steamers, and finally banks and railroads. Well, everything seemed unworthy of a cartoonist's attention thus far.

Notice the dollar signs on Hanna's trousers. Davenport never showed his quarry partial to any other kind of design, as if reminding his readers that money was the root of all evil.

Mr. Hanna's Stand on the Labor Question.

However, in 1880 Mark Hanna started becoming active within the Republican Party in Cleveland, and shortly after began an association with politician William McKinley at the next two Republican national conventions. Following these came the fruition of it all in 1896: McKinley won the Republican nomination for the Presidency, under the personal management of Hanna. Some months later, it was Hanna whose skill guided the nominee into the White House, running against William Jennings

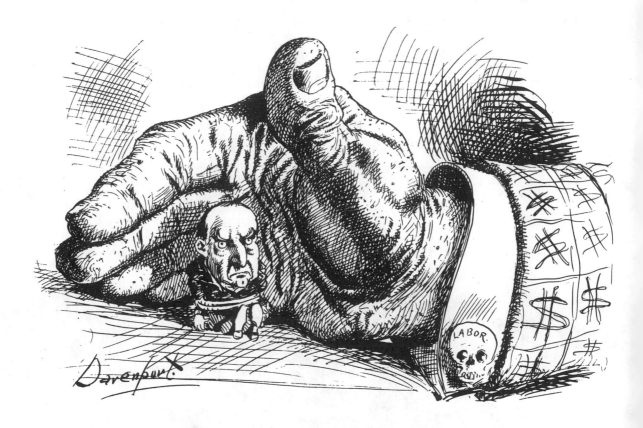

A Man Of Mark.

Bryan on the issue of "free silver." Unfortunately for both the new President and his mentor, however, very powerful forces remained opposed to both of them, including publisher Hearst, whose own political aspirations were well known.

In the above cartoon Hanna had a jacket to match those trousers. Note also that the type of hand Davenport used in this drawing looks like one that could squeeze blood out of a stone.

In this cartoon, we are left with the feeling that even after those two horses go galloping off the page into the distance, or as far as polo ponies will travel, we will still remember the wonderful crosshatch, pen-and-ink technique used by the artist.

Frederick Burr Opper (1857-1937) was another great talent drafted by publisher Hearst for the war against Hanna and McKinley. One of America's most prolific cartoonists, his successes in the comic-strip field included "Happy Hooligan," "Alphonse and Gaston," "Si and Maude," and "Our Antediluvian Ancestors."

"Now, Willie, you and Teddy can have a nice game of peek-a-boo. Papa likes to see little boys enjoy themselves.

Everything in this cartoon is designed for easy interpretation by the newspaper reader, so that he can chuckle at it over the breakfast table with his wife, or at the office with his fellow-workers—"the Trusts," fat and swollen (with profits, of course); Teddy Roosevelt and "Willie" McKinley neatly tucked away in his pockets; and "Mama" Hanna looking on approvingly at the whole happy scene.

Part of a long-running series, Opper wisely kept these same characters "moving around," not because he knew they'd be published in book form eventually, or thought readers had long memories, but simply to keep the work interesting for himself. Possibly, had the series lasted long enough, readers might have seen "Willie and his Papa" in a view from the ceiling, à la film director Busby Berkeley.

Bigger and broader grew Opper's figures of "the Trusts" (and his wife), more and more wizened the two mortal enemies of Hearst, who had favored William Jennings Bryan for the Presidency.

"YES, WILLIE, WE WILL HAVE A LITTLE DRILL IN MILITARISM. PAPA IS GOING TO HAVE A LARGE STANDING ARMY, IF THE ELECTION GOES AS PAPA HOPES. PAPA NEEDS IT IN HIS BUSINESS. 'TEN-SHUN!'"

In this cartoon, Opper even gave his readers an extra laugh at T.R.'s expense, ridiculing the famous Spanish-American War "Rough Rider" of San Juan Hill.

"YES, WILLIE, THIS IS THE NEW SUIT PAPA EXPECTS TO WEAR. THERE WON'T BE ANY UNCLE SAM BUT PAPA, WHEN PAPA HAS GRABBED THE WHOLE COUNTRY."

Thomas E. Powers (1870-1939), still another cartoonist recruited by Hearst during the circulation wars with Joseph Pulitzer and other publishers, might not have known how to spell "Monroe," but he certainly was no slouch when it came to making Uncle Sam look like the "good guy" and foreigners look like the personification of everything evil—a far cry from the political cartoonist of today who must think carefully before vilifying *anybody* on account of racial characteristics. Powers held his job with the Hearst newspapers for upward of 30 years and, for what he was supposed to do, he did it well. This cartoon, propaganda for Hearst's "yellow peril" line, is intended to frighten readers out of their wits at the prospect of a Japanese take-over of the Western Hemisphere. Why, that "Mexican" fisherman is even using bullets for bait! (Incidentally, the "Uncle Sam" Powers drew was partially developed by Thomas Nast who, as previously noted, was foreign-born himself!)

The Spanish-American War of 1898 produced symbols that were almost sacrosanct. Uncle Sam became like Paul Bunyan, swinging an axe at other continents; or he was shown in the act of lighting a bomb that could set off a whole chain reaction around the world; but always, as we see, he must do these things with an air of inifinite wisdom. Even the bald eagle must appear beyond reproach, hardly capable of entertaining dastardly ideas like swooping down and carrying off little babies, quite a statesman, or states-bird, himself. Below are two rather benign views of the war by R.C. Bowman that appeared in the Minneapolis *Tribune*.

Uncle Sam's next duty.

J. BULL—" Boys, it strikes us that bird has grown a bit."

Three more cartoons of Spanish-American War vintage, showing Uncle Sam fearless and invincible, if a little pushy; Uncle Sam even more courageous than a Chief Executive; and an explosion in the nation's capitol which seemed propitious at the moment, since the enemy was reported to have just blown up one of our battleships (the *Maine*) in the harbor at Havana.

Uncle Sam's string of cannon crackers.

UNCLE SAM—"All that you need is backbone."

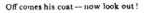

Off comes his coat — now look out !

THE 20th CENTURY

National Emergencies, real or manufactured, are often an excuse to make anything happen; a President can become even bigger that all the symbols and emblems of a country, as the political cartoonist Walker portrayed Theodore Roosevelt in this cartoon.

There is nothing more likely to speed a cartoonist to his drawing board than a political scandal. Below political cartoonist T.S. Sullivant exposes tycoon Thomas Fortune Ryan for sabotaging the construction of the Panama Canal by luring away key Canal people to work instead for his private railroad interests.

THE NEW NATIONALISM
"DO YOU FOLLOW ME, SAM?"

Art Young (1866-1943) apparently subscribed to the theory that if war is hell, so is the planet Earth. He was arrested under the Espionage Act, along with the editors of the *Masses* in 1917, for doing a cartoon against the war. (The trial eventually ended in a hung jury.) He also produced a book of drawings to illustrate his point of view, calling it *Art Young's Inferno*. Of course, it wasn't the nether world below that readers were asked to examine by the cartoonist, but the one they already inhabited.

Again, we can see the important part emotion plays in a political cartoonist's work! Young's baby (above) is a creature of tenderness and love, as are even his adult nudes. All else, the hellion creature and the city and its slums, are drawn with hate and fury.

SOOTY CITIES

SLUMS

Less emotional here, Young is concerned with making these humans see themselves as fools and pawns, literally stripping them of their dignity.

GRAFT

STOCK EXCHANGE

FFICE OF

LES G. DAWES

The Minute Man
Costume of 1776

Young

A "radical" cartoon by Young, of a future Vice President of the United States, revealed banker Charles G. Dawes, who volunteered for active duty in 1917 and rose quickly to brigadier general, in charge of all purchasing for the U.S. Army.

Rollin Kirby (1875-1952) is credited by admirers with effecting the repeal of an amendment to the U.S. Constitution. In 1919, over the veto of President Wilson, Congress passed a law to enforce the recently ratified Eighteenth Amendment (Prohibition). This law, known as the Volstead Act, (named after a Congressman from Minnesota), prohibited the sale of intoxicating liquors, which it defined as containing "one half of one percent or more of alcohol by volume." The Volstead Act and even the Amendment were roundly attacked by many who foresaw that only the underworld would gain from it, and a fight began for the repeal of Prohibition that lasted until the administration of Franklin Delano Roosevelt in 1933. The high watermark of this period, from the standpoint of political cartooning, was the emergence of Rollin Kirby's "Mr. Dry." Notice how brilliantly conceived this figure was, deadly and sepulchral, yet comical and amusing at the same time.

"NOW THEN, ALL TOGETHER, 'MY COUNTRY 'TIS OF THEE'"

Of course, from coast to coast, other cartoonists joined in the great crusade against Prohibition, as deaths and tragedies from the sale of illegal liquor and the anticipated gangland infiltration of high places in government increased.

THE LAST BIG OFFENSIVE

However, it is universally recognized that Kirby's cartoon contribution to the cause was the greatest of all, and even after Repeal finally became a reality, many newspaper readers continued to miss seeing "Mr. Dry."

Franklin Delano Roosevelt took office in 1933, at the depth of an unprecedented economic crisis still remembered as the Great Depression. His administration was regarded as either a period of monumental achievements or the worst calamity that ever hit a nation, as he set about issuing proclamations closing banks, embargoing gold, and getting Congress to establish such agencies as a National Recovery Administration, a Civilian Conservation Corps, and federal relief for the needy. In short, F.D.R. made himself fair game for the editorial pages, and remained so until his death in 1945, almost at the end of World War II.

When a political cartoonist is on the side of a Chief Executive, or anyone else, the subject is depicted as kind and considerate, and the treatment is even flattering. "Beauty is in the eyes of the beholder," as the old saying goes, and if the cartoonist sees features that cannot be flattered, he disregards them. As seen through the eyes of Rollin Kirby, who won three Pulitzer prizes in his lifetime, President Roosevelt was a fine man, a handsome man, a man whose face certainly belonged right up there on Mt. Rushmore alongside those other Presidents with nice faces.

MAKERS OF HISTORY

In the mid-1930's armed gangs roamed the streets of New York, incited to violence by radio demagogues, one of them in particular a "man of the cloth," shouting racial slurs and vituperations against the government, and assaulting peaceful citizens. Out in the suburbs of Long Island and New Jersey, too, uniformed followers of Adolf Hitler had set up camps where they marched in goose-step fashion, reiterating their allegiance to the Third Reich, Apparently, this was more than Illinois-born Rollin Kirby could tolerate in the city he loved so much.

Not a particularly great idea as political cartoons go, perhaps, but Kirby made this one work nevertheless. "Here is what is going on," he told his readers. "Here is the kind of person who is trying to take over our city, our state, our country. Here is the flag he wishes to make our flag. What shall *we* do about it?"

A final blockbuster cartoon by Rollin Kirby, created on the occasion of an announcement by Adolf Hitler of a secret weapon for accomplishing the quick defeat of the U.S.S.R. and an end to all resistance.

THINK FAST, ADOLF!

The implements used by Kirby here were simple: a statement of Great Britain's Prime Minister, an excellent likeness of Nazi Germany's Führer, the aforesaid "secret weapon," and lastly, a snappy bit of advice by the political cartoonist himself!

Boardman Robinson (1876-1952), born in Nova Scotia, the son of a sea captain, Robinson studied art in Boston and Paris, then found employment on the staff of the New York *Morning Telegram.* "A greater artist than Robert Minor, but not so great a political cartoonist," was the way Fitzpatrick described this giant of the profession. In 1914, shortly after the outbreak of the first World War, this gifted cartoonist, illustrator, and painter, who eventually became an instructor at the Art Students League in New York, made an important decision—to accompany the noted war correspondent John Reed on a tour of Europe.

In this drawing, a protest against the (then) complete lack of welfare for the needy, Robinson's juxtaposition of light and dark is extremely effective, a mere few lines being used to suggest the slum background.

RUSSIA SURROUNDED, 1918

Spotlighting an obscure page in history, the Allies, together with their erstwhile enemy, Germany, are shown as beasts attempting to attack the "virgin socialist country."

Reed, according to Barbara Gelb in her biography *So Short A Time*, "wrote skillfully about the war—not with detachment, but with the clarity and compassion of the engaged and articulate journalist." He had already expressed disillusionment with the fighting. "The truth is that with two millions of the youth of France fighting a losing battle against the German hordes pouring down from the North, Paris, the heart and soul of France, remained tranquil, ignorant, apathetic," he wrote for the magazine *Metropolitan*. Describing how wealthy homes and hotels had been turned over to the Red Cross only to save them from destruction, and how business in the city was going on as usual, Reed stated in an article for the *Masses*, "this is not our war."

Even in this somewhat uninspired cartoon, Robinson proved his mastery, showing a British newspaper attempting to protect Raymond Poincaré, President of the French Republic, who has been trying to sabotage trade relations between the two nations.

Masterly draftsmanship makes this an unforgettable picture—the beautifully drawn Christ, the powerful figures of workers storming the bastion.

THE SECOND COMING

On a battleground where the Serbian and Austrian armies had recently faced each other, John Reed provided more horrifying detail: "On one side . . . were the Serbian trenches, on the other side the Austrian. Barely twenty yards separated the two. Here and there both trenches merged into immense pits, forty feet around and fifty feet deep, where the enemy had undermined and dynamited them. The ground between was humped into irregular piles of earth, Looking closer, we saw a ghastly thing: from these little mounds protruded pieces of uniform, skulls with draggled hair, upon which shreds of flesh still hung; white bones with rotting hands at the end, bloody bones sticking from boots. . . .

"We walked on the dead, so thick were they—sometimes our feet sank through into pits of rotting flesh, crunching bones. Little holes opened suddenly, leading deep down and swarming with gray maggots. . . ."

One of the most powerful satirical cartoons of all times, is this Boardman Robinson conception of the Masters of the Universe, none other than the Earth's own war lords, being serenaded by angels while down below the downtrodden mass their forces in, perhaps, a futile resistance.

"GOD"

Robert Minor (1884-1952), son of a Texas judge might earn a prize for the most frustrated artist of all time. Employed for many years by many newspapers, including the St, Louis *Post-Dispatch* (which he left in 1913), Minor was called "the greatest political cartoonist of all time" by none other than Daniel R. Fitzpatrick, certainly one of the all-time greats himself. Pioneering in the bold, heavy style that featured using the flat end of a lithograph crayon, Minor abruptly called a halt to his professional career

during World War I in order to join the Communist Party and devote the rest of his life to writing pamphlets, lecturing, organizing within the labor movement, and campaigning vainly for public office. One can't help wondering if "Fighting Bob" ever nurtured a secret dream of returning to his old drawing board.

The powerful physical development of the Army recruit was intended, of course, to give the anti-war elements a feeling of strength. It goes without saying that a hawk cartoonist of the same period would have put a head on that figure and made him look absolutely *eager* to go overseas.

Army Medical Examiner: "At last a perfect soldier!"

James T. Alley (1885-1934), cartoonist for the Memphis *Commercial Appeal*, appeared at times disillusioned with both U.S. political parties. The Teapot Dome Scandal (the Watergate of the 1920s), during the Administration of Warren G. Harding, revealed extensive political corruption in Washington and increased Alley's disillusionment with the parties.

Oh, Boy!

Here Alley struck a blow for penitentiary reform.

Enlightened Society's Representative On The Job!

Here he only wished the GOP could beat a path through that jungle!

He Never Was an Explorer

Like his co-worker in the South, "Spang" of the Montgomery (Alabama) *Advertiser,* Jim Alley, producing political cartoons in Memphis, Tennessee, loathed groups attempting to spread doctrines of race hatred across the land. Born in Sidell, Arkansas, a small town near Little Rock, he saw similarity in the philosophy of the racists with that of the National Socialist (Nazi) Party of Germany, whose leader Adolf Hitler had already vowed in his book *Mein Kampf,* a world bloodbath.

Much of political cartooning is wishful thinking. Here, Jim Alley had the Klan ragged and poor, practically down-and-out in a period when it was still powerful and influential; Hitler himself appears to be merely a ridiculous strutting midget, seemingly incapable of ever attaining appreciable growth and becoming a menace to free men everywhere.

Louis Dalrymple (1866-1905), of the old *Puck* and other publications captures Republican leader Thomas Platt in the still of the night, having just burgled a nice little GOP-type girl of a sackful of goodies that could only gain him more influence in the party. Note that Platt's "jimmy" has New York Governor Charles Evans Hughes on its head, and that the little girl's rug is terribly peeved about all this.

Frank ("Spang") Spangler (1881-1946) could be warm and tender, and cold and hard. Nobody experiences such contrasting moods more than a political cartoonist who, by the very nature of his profession, has emotions that keep changing with the news of the day. For example, take the issue of human survival. If he feels deeply about other people's lives, holocausts and mass tragedies will affect him as if he and his own loved ones are personally involved. Frank Spangler demonstrated this on the occasion of one of the worst disasters ever to take place at sea, the sinking of the *Titanic* in the North Atlantic, on her maiden voyage.

$---Orders!---$

We can sense, in this drawing, the pen of "Spang" moving almost blindly over the paper, thrashing it in despair as he brought home to his readers, somehow, the feeling of the cold, murky water that April night in 1912. Indeed, so steeped in grief must Frank Spangler have been over the fate of the *Titanic* and its hundreds of lost souls, that he flatly rejected the official explanation of the vessel hitting an iceberg, preferring to torture himself with the notion that "greed" was to blame.

We now see another side of Frank Spangler, one in which he is full of angry indictment. The issue is civil rights and he is dealing with a hate group—the Ku Klux Klan—that roams the countryside, preying on defenseless individuals and their families. The culprit, in this case, is the Honorable Thomas J. Heflin, Republican Senator from the state of Alabama, a self-proclaimed member of the Klan, who repeatedly stated that he "would support whole-heartedly any move to suppress blacks, Jews, and Catholics," both at clandestine meetings of the Klan itself, or right on the floor of the United States Senate. The attempt by Governor Alfred E. Smith of New York to win the Democratic nomination for President, was "a plot of the Catholic hierarchy in Rome," declared Heflin in statements to the press many times in the late 1920's.

Having His Hand McCalled—   —Spang

In this drawing, hailing a legal decree against the Ku Klux Klan, "Spang" has drawn a distorted human figure. Why such grotesquerie from one whose competence as an artist had been proven hundreds of times before? The answer is obvious: The political cartoonist wanted his readers to share his revulsion for the Klan, to hate it as he did!

To carry on this fight almost single-handedly in the "deep South" took great courage on the part of Frank Spangler. His newspaper, the Montgomery (Alabama) *Advertiser*, deserved equal credit for its support of such a crusade.

he Filling Station —Spang

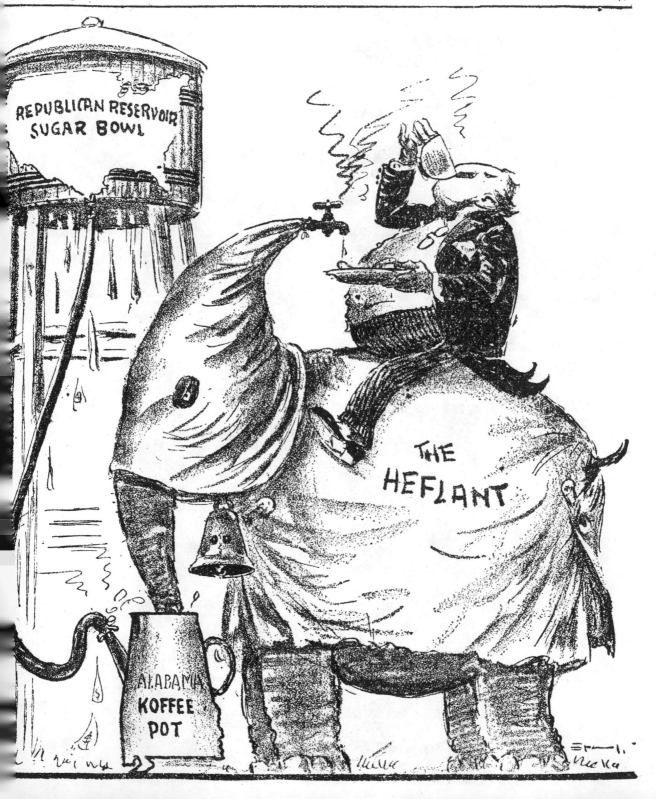

Like Nast with Boss Tweed and Opper with "Willie and his Papa," Frank Spangler had to keep his long series against Heflin and the Klan fresh and exciting all the time it was running. He did this with a variety of situations, some funny, some serious, but all in dead earnest.

"Helfant," "Heflivver," "Heflincubator"—Spang even used puns to keep his readers amused—*and angry!*

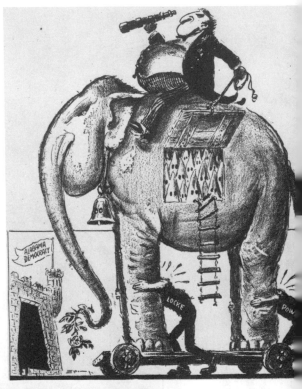

Daniel R. Fitzpatrick (1891-1969), was the genius who came into being at the St. Louis *Post-Dispatch*, in 1913, inheriting his job from Robert Minor. Born in Superior, Wisconsin, Fitzpatrick attended the Art Institute of Chicago, then started his professional career with the *Daily News* in that city. Hired by the St. Louis paper at the age of 22, Fitz, early in his career, drew the typical large heads and tiny bodies of those times, eventually developing a style of his own following the inevitable period of showing the influence of Minor and Boardman Robinson, to the extent that he won the Pulitzer prize in 1926 (refusing to submit any more entries for the award after that.) One of the most remarkable things about Daniel Fitzpatrick's career was the complete independence he enjoyed with his paper throughout his long association with it, choosing to lay down his crayon when the St. Louis Post-Dispatch supported Republican Alf Landon against Roosevelt in 1936, and again, "going fishing" when Thomas Dewey received its support in 1948. Never topping more than 127 pounds

SHORT OF WAR MEANS WHAT IT SAYS TO WILLIAM ALLEN WHITE.

© St. Louis Post-Dispatch

of weight on his five-foot eleven-inch frame, Fitz conceded when he finally retired after 45 years of doing some of the most powerful political cartoons in the history of the profession, that he had "made a lot of people goddam mad."

Ten months before the Japanese attack on Pearl Harbor (and even after), the American nation was sharply divided into two camps, one, certain that Hitler, who had already annexed much of Europe, had to be stopped in his tracks now; the other, isolationist and insisting that what went on abroad was no concern of ours. The great, slashing crayon of Fitzpatrick seemed to make short work of the latter group in the cartoon on the previous page showing the isolationists, along with everything else, about to be consumed by one of the most frightening skulls ever drawn.

Borrowing Nast's idea of a dollar bag on the head of a Tammany boss, Fitzpatrick went it one better, creating this "45¢-a-day" face to represent

DIRECT RELIEF IN MISSOURI.

ALL IN THE NAME OF THE FOUR FREEDOMS.

the exact sum of money needy persons in his own state were receiving to sustain themselves and their families during the Depression. Again, that mighty crayon did the job, capturing the degradation of an American home and family.

President Roosevelt had proclaimed the Four Freedoms of every American citizen: freedom of speech and of worship; freedom from want and from fear. Attacking federal investigative agencies, in the news even at that time for illegal bugging, Fitz was politely but firmly inquiring if this too was one of the freedoms. It's interesting to note that the cartoonist just naturally seemed to prefer drawing low-income-type homes, like the one shown here.

That crayon, already immortal in so many of Dan Fitzpatrick's drawings, brought home most dramatically, as no printed word could do, and perhaps no other cartoonist, the horrible fate that had befallen still another nation caught in the ruthless path of the Nazi juggernaut. (Although occupied by the Nazis, Yugoslavia did not in fact join the Axis.)

YUGOSLAVIA JOINS THE AXIS.

© St. Louis Post-Dispatch

A three-point landing for readers' eyes: one, the swastika ball and chain; two, the beaten, bowed people of Italy; and three, that fat-bellied vulture perched on the remains of a classic column. This is how Fitz related the tragedy of a great nation under Benito Mussolini.

THE GRANDEUR THAT WAS ROME.

William Gropper born in 1897 on New York's lower East Side, with its pioneer immigrants and sweatshops, began work at a very young age to help the family meet its budget needs. A passerby one day chanced to see some of the boy's drawings on a wall or sidewalk and recommended him for an art school, one that happened to have Robert Henri and George Bellows as overseers, and where Robert Minor turned out to be a student. Eventually, Gropper succeeded in winning a scholarship to the National Academy of Design, and shortly afterward his drawings came to the attention of an alert New York *Tribune* editor who quickly hired him as a sketch reporter. One day the paper sent Gropper out to cover a meeting of the radical International Workers of the World (Wobblies). All the talk

War

about a "class struggle" changed Gropper's thinking drastically, seeming to offer him answers he had been seeking. He stayed and joined the movement himself, doing posters, drawings, and illustrations for the "revolutionary" press. Beginning in 1924, Gropper did a daily political cartoon for the Yiddish newspaper *Freiheit*, as well as for the weekly *New Masses*, but his work caught the discerning eyes of editors of such glossies as *The New Yorker* and *Vanity Fair* as well. Before long, the cartoonist was on his way to international fame.

There was no doubt how Gropper felt about Armageddon where his country was concerned, or about certain people who stood to profit from it. It's interesting to contemplate the effect of political cartoons on top hats and swallow-tail coats as *popular* wearing apparel.

Gropper's early fear that current events indicated the coming of World War II is shown here.

Next War

1914

1927

One of the fastest cartoonists on record, Bill Gropper could do a drawing like this in three minutes. Perhaps that was as long as he would look at a "warmonger."

This cartoon of the Emperor of Japan, done six years prior to Pearl Harbor, had international repercussions; the U.S. State Department issued a disclaimer. The folding of *Vanity Fair* soon after the incident was blamed on pressure by the Japanese government on U.S. business firms to withdraw their advertising.

JAPAN'S EMPEROR GETS THE NOBEL PEACE PRIZE

Compare Rollin Kirby's likeness of F.D.R. with this caricature of the World War II president.

Tom Little (1898-1972) cartoonist of the *Tennessean* was a member of the profession who could certainly draw with bitterness sometimes, and with affection other times. Here, in a study of F.D.R. during World War II, we have an example of Little with lots of affection.

© The Tennyssean

That skipper is Roosevelt, pure and simple, the hand clutching the wheel somewhat exaggerated in size in order to lend it strength.

Here we have Tom Little in reverse, caricaturing with bitterness the titular head of an organization noted for its racist philosophy. Note that none of the clichés normally associated with bigots have been overlooked by the political cartoonist—the thin lips, the unyielding expression, the skull seemingly carved from granite, and of course, a weapon that was very popular back in the age of the Neanderthals.

Incredible as it seems, before Little became anchored to a drawing board, he worked on his paper for 21 years as a police reporter, general assignment man, and city editor!

"I'LL TELL YOU HOW TO RUN THE COUNTRY!"

A description cartoonist Charles Bissell once offered about his late brother-in-law's daily agony at "getting started," probably fits political cartoonist the world over: "Tom's day at the *Tennessean* begins with the morning grouch sustained anywhere from 7:30 to 3 o'clock. Getting a cartoon idea, particularly a funny one, is a grim and terrible business, and Tom makes the worst of it. He does a lot of earnest reading and quite a bit of restless wandering about the office. He tries this desk and that desk and adjusts his hat at a hundred or so different angles. His face, at such times, is no pleasant sight, for written across it are more different expressions than one face can comfortably contain. There is of course, the pained look that upon all faces is the accepted expression of thought, but also commingled there are looks of suspicion, greed, intolerance, cruelty, shame, fatuity, friendship, mirth and murder. The explanation for this lively state of face is simply that as cartoon ideas occur to him he assumes the facial expressions of the characters in them who, as a rule, are in unpleasant, embarrassing or deplorable circumstances. Out of this struggle there invariably comes an idea and when he's got it he goes upstairs and gets to work. If he is pleased with his idea he takes off his hat, lights his pipe and becomes as nice a guy as you would want to know—but when you see him at his board with his hat pulled down over his eyes, look out."

This cartoon won Tom Little a Pulitzer Prize in 1957, certainly well-deserved for its fine sympathetic drawing and promotion of a much-needed vaccine.

Equally appealing was this classic drawing stressing medical aid for the elderly.

"I WONDER WHY MY PARENTS DIDN'T GIVE ME SALK SHOTS?"

Clarence D. ("Batch") Batchelor retired cartoonist for the *New York News* drew a beautifully hideous woman representing Death as the symbol for war. Winning a Pulitzer prize for one such "lady," Batch did lots more, this one perhaps modeled after Millet's famous painting *The Sowers*.

Arthur Szyk (1894-1951), undoubtedly one of the 20th century's outstanding political caricaturists, conveys his emotional outrage in a drawing of a Japanese officer made soon after the attack on Pearl Harbor.

David Low (1891-1963). To many people, in England particularly, World War II is remembered as a private war between David Low on the one hand and Hitler and Mussolini on the other, so influential was this cartoonist's work from 1939 to 1946, although his distinguished career had begun years before and lasted well after the war's end.

Born in New Zealand, Low, without a single artist adorning his family tree, first became attracted to cartooning as a child by reading "halfpenny comics" starring such characters as "Weary Willy and Tired Tim," and "Airy Alfy and Bouncing Billy." Endeavoring to improve his own drawing skills, he subscribed to a correspondence art school thousands of miles away in New York City, at a dollar a month.

Graduating to more refined tastes, Low was attracted to the pages of *Punch*, where he found inspiration in the works of Keene, Sambourne, Caldecott, and Gibson. Then, beginning with police-court sketching for local papers, to extend his experiences "both as an artist and a human being," he eventually acquired the position of staff political cartoonist with the *Spectator* in Christchurch, New Zealand, and in 1911 with the *Bulletin*, in Sydney, Australia.

Low might have anticipated a protest from the lower order of the species when he did this World War II cartoon.

"HE ASKED FOR PEACE"

RENDEZVOUS

Splendidly drawn as ever, two adversaries meet face-to-face on a World War II battlefield.

With the outbreak of World War I, David Low was "by no means convinced of the total wrongness of Germany's claim to a place in the sun," according to his 1957 autobiography published by Simon & Schuster. Working closely with Norman Lindsay on the *Bulletin*, he twitted America's Woodrow Wilson as well as the Kaiser, and narrowly escaped being called up for military service himself on the grounds of "national importance."

Having already established a world-wide reputation in his field, via multitudinous reprints of his drawings, it was inevitable that David Low would receive an invitation to work in England. In 1919 he came to work for the London *Star*, and in 1927 changed to the London *Evening Standard*.

In England, Low's popularity continued to grow both at home and abroad. He became an intimate friend and confidant of kings, prime ministers, and heads of state everywhere. As a growing liberal, he was responsible for such unforgettable cartoons as "Lloyd George and the Double-headed Ass," a not too gentle commentary on Liberal and Conservative party rivalries; and "Progress to Liberty-Amristar Style," a strong attack on colonialism as it affected Ireland and India.

THE WORST CAUSE IN THE WORLD
(WITH THE BEST PROPAGANDA)

THE BEST CAUSE IN THE WORLD
(WITH THE WORST PROPAGANDA)

PROPAGANDA

A Low cartoon lampooning the ineffectiveness of his own country's propaganda machine compared to that of the enemy.

World War II may have resulted in a stringent diet for the English people, but David Low saw to it that they continued to be fed a steady diet of humor. His comic strip "Hit and Muss," a sort of Mutt and Jeff treatment of Hitler and Mussolini, alternated with characters like "Colonel Blimp," the lovable old duffer forever uttering self-contradictory aphorisms ("Gad, sir, Mr. Lansbury is right. The League of Nations should insist on peace—except, of course, in the event of war.") kept readers in a constant state of amusement and their morale jolly well good, indeed.

An excellent caricaturist, Low's subjects included every luminary who ever made the news, from France's Marshall Foch to his own country's Neville Chamberlain, whose face somehow became part of that individual's famous umbrella. But most felt flattered, few outraged. Sigmund Freud once wrote to Low, "A Jewish refugee from Vienna, a very old man personally and unknown to you, cannot resist the impulse to tell you how much he admires your glorious art and your inexorable, unfailing criticism."

Women's Rights. As the Equal Rights Amendment to the Constitution still appears uncertain of adoption it is interesting to note that most political cartoonists were always in the ladies' corner.

The Martyr

The age of chivalry was not quite dead as Rollin Kirby and other editorial cartoonists joined the ladies in their struggle for liberation.

The boys, naturally, were still regarding them as "sex objects," judging by the twinkle in their eyes in this cartoon by William Chamberlain.

The triumphal march

CASSEL

Packing His Belongings

Naturally, too, the issue of women's lib was uppermost in the minds of politicians such as New York State Governor and soon-to-be Secretary of State Charles Evans Hughes, as they swung around the country on "whistle stops."

This cartoon was unique because it was done by a lady! Nine E. Allender had a long and distinguished career as a political cartoonist.

Chorus of Politicians: "Carry your luggage, lady?"

No less a person than President Woodrow Wilson staunchly refused to have an eye for the ladies, at least in this cartoon—

SCOTT in Cleveland Leader   The Cut Direct

——but it made a difference, as this cartoon demonstrates, when the prize was votes—now Democrats and Republicans alike dived in to win the ladies' favors.

It makes a difference!

War Cartoons. Cartoons were not always slashing attacks on militarism. Some were rather whimsical comments on man's most irrational behavior. Political cartoonists greeted hostilities between nations with varying degrees of emotion.

Jim Alley's assignment: to make Kaiser Wilhelm look like he wasn't quite big enough to take on the Allies.

is 1914 Outfit, August 6, 1918

Cliff Berryman, in this picture anyway, chose to make the whole bloody conflict seem like just another news item.

Bellona, the wife or sister of Mars, herself a Roman goddess of war, whose temple was dedicated during a battle between the Samnites and Etruscans in 296 B.C., is drawn as quite a *guy* herself as "she" comforts the Kaiser in this beautiful drawing by Australia's Norman Lindsay.

The cartoonist apparently believed that at Bellona's temple priests conducted fanatical rites that included drinking the blood of their victims. Judging by Kaiser Wilhelm's worried expression, he was aware of this, too.

THE DANGEROUS YEAR

Bellona (in the fourth year of marriage):   "And do you still love me as you did before we married?"

ORD: "Where have you been this time? London, Paris, Warsaw, or Rome?"

ZEPPELIN: "I don't know. It's not in der papers!"

The Kaiser again, this time confused himself by England's handling of the news media.

In time of war, comic artists may suddenly become political cartoonists. Clare Briggs was the creator of "When a Feller Needs a Friend," and this is one of the "fellers" lending a hand in the cause of civilian mobilization.

INTRODUCING "SKIN-NAY"
This is the First Time He's ever "Come Over"

Advice and Consent. Did President Richard Nixon have a hard time "packing" the Supreme Court in 1969 and 1970? In the above cartoon by John Chase, we see that Franklin D. Roosevelt had no picnic either. Stanley Reed served on the Supreme Court from 1938 to 1957.

THE MODERNS/
United States and Canada

Cal Alley (1915-1970), son of Pulitzer prizewinning editorial cartoonist James T. Alley, inherited his father's job on the *Commercial Appeal* at the age of 30, using the same cigarette-burned pen-pocked drawing board as his dad. But Cal didn't have to trade on his father's reputation. He had enough compassion and talent to make it on his own.

"Welcome"

Winner of innumerable awards for his editorial cartoons, and creator of a well-remembered comic strip, "The Ryatts," Memphis-born Cal attended the Academy of Arts in that city, as well as the Chicago Academy, and was formerly connected with the now-defunct Kansas City *Journal*.

Affluent America

The figure was the same one his father had drawn before him, but shades of '29 and the Great Depression, how prices had changed!

"Get Off My Back!!"

Was the guy on the floor fed up with being treated like a dumb bunny? Alley made him appear capable of unloading that burden on his back, if he didn't already have a hernia.

Blame The Piper . . . Not The Kids

People were up in arms hollering about the youth of the country. In this drawing, Cal Alley simply asked that people take a look at who was leading them.

IN THE 'CLUTCHES' OF THE LAW

Striking out at the coddling of hate groups, Cal Alley clearly showed that he was continuing a great heritage, following in the path set for him by his father.

Ed Ashley was born in Milan, Ohio, the birthplace of Thomas Edison, but he says it was too late for him to lend a hand helping invent the electric bulb.

Ashley attended Toledo University, served in the U.S. Army Air Force during World War II, then took up the study of art at Pratt University in Brooklyn, N.Y., graduating in 1953. After that, there were a dozen years in Colorado, some of them spent in the advertising department of the Denver *Post*, before he joined the Toledo (Ohio) *Blade*.

... AND CARRY A BIG STICK

'NEVER MIND THE BAG.. I'LL JUST PUT 'EM IN MY PURSE'

Inflation was sending the price of consumer goods skyrocketing. Where else could Ashley find better proof of this than at the checkout counter of his local supermarket?

Here he takes a crack at a couple of innocent by-standers during the fuel "shortage" that followed the Middle East war in 1973.

FOR THE LIFE OF ME, I CAN'T UNDERSTAND WHAT'S SO IMPORTANT ABOUT GASOLINE

As we shall see, Ed Ashley's pattern of life corresponds with most contemporary editorial cartoonists. In Ashley's case, he draws up one or two ideas a day for approval by his editors. Then, having achieved an okay, he proceeds to do his finished drawing right at the paper, in a small office which he describes as "a phone booth with ink stains."

Ashley's principal weapons are two-ply, medium surface Strathmore paper; Artsign Finepoint No. 5 brushes; Prismacolor 935 black crayons and, of course, india ink. An average finish takes him about two hours.

As for occasional disagreements with his editor over ideas, Ashley says, "I'm lucky enough to work for a liberal paper with editors I consider to be flexible and intelligent. I can't imagine being employed by a paper with a philosophy diametrically opposed to mine."

Tony Auth, a native of southern California, practically grew up in a sick-bed as a child, and spent hours illustrating radio dramas as they came over the air. Graduating from UCLA, he worked briefly as a medical illustrator and got interested in politics during the Vietnam War. He landed his job by besieging newspapers for employment until the publisher of the Philadelphia *Inquirer* hired him.

Auth assiduously avoids socializing with politicians for fear he might one day have to make a drawing about them. "When anyone wants to be a social critic, it's detrimental to become friends with the people you may be criticizing," he says. "For instance, our mayor here in Philadelphia is a very dynamic, magnetic personality, and it would be almost impossible not to like him personally. But if I were to become buddies with him, that might prove to be a serious handicap for me."

'He's trying to save face.'

Detente

Above, Auth showed the two greatest powers on earth having reached a "perfect" understanding.

What do little children ask for Christmas? A little President Nixon asked only that people believe in him.

'You can visit your wife now, sir . . . sir?'

Mounting hospital expenses concerned the editorial cartoonist here. In this case, he was concerned with a world in which one day air-traveler St. Nick himself might be subjected to a frisk.

How does Tony Auth work with his paper? "My arrangement with my editor is that no one at the paper will tell me what to draw, but, on the other hand, they have veto power. I recognize that this compromise is a realistic one, and necessary right now, between the desire on the part of an artist for autonomy, and the desire of a paper to have the artist be the graphic voice of the editorial page."

Sometimes an editorial cartoon doesn't need a title, as we may see by this one on a high-priority topic.

Sometimes it doesn't even need a cartoon! Auth drew this as the Senate Watergate Committee introduced charts attempting to explain the working relationship between members of the White House staff.

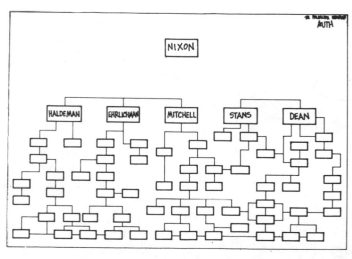

Tony Auth says, "My 'roughs' have always been very fast. When doing them, I never worry about style—just about getting an idea down on paper that works. For the past year or so, I've been using a light box and tracing my roughs for the finished art. So my 'style' is, I think, much more natural and spontaneous.

"I use Grafix paper and I try to achieve the effect of a wash drawing. To do that, I apply the developer with a variety of materials: sponges, clothes, brush, dry brush, etc. As far as pens go, I use mainly a double zero and number one Repitograph, a number 290 and number 303 Gillotte, and assorted ball-points and felt tips.

"I do about half my work at home and half at the paper. At 9:30 every morning, I show the editor whatever I have and would like to be drawing that day. He picks what he thinks is best and I do that one. Occasionally there is debate and if I have a cartoon I really want to do and the editor refuses to publish it, I have the option of doing it and syndicating it, without the *Inquirer* copyright line."

This is a rough.

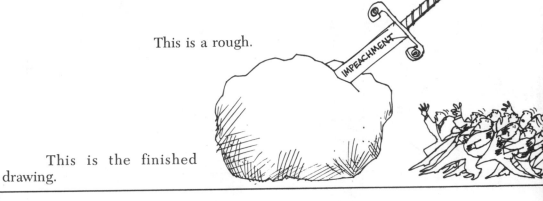

This is the finished drawing.

Cliff ("Baldy") Baldowski appears on the editorial pages of the Atlanta *Constitution* seven days a week. A former Air Force navigator and intelligence officer, he received training in drawing at the Art Students League in New York City.

In 1963, "Baldy" compiled a book of cartoons on civil rights for the International Council on Human Relations. In 1965, the National Council of Parents and Teachers honored him for his work on school dropouts.

A product of Augusta, Georgia, he received the 1971 Freedoms Foundation Medal, presented at Valley Forge, Pennsylvania.

"Y'ALL ABOUT READY—?"

"Don't expect much help from *me*," Baldy's average guy seems to be saying, perhaps voicing a cynicism shared by many of his fellow citizens in the wake of national political scandals.

In this editorial cartoon, Cliff Baldowski gave his readers an up-to-the minute report on the very latest kind of space journey currently in progress.

"DON'T EXPLAIN IT, JUST DRIVE. . ."

Jim Bensfield, a part-time editorial cartoonist, became a practicing attorney in Washington, D.C. A compulsive artist who has illustrated many children's books, he wonders why he ever attended Harvard Law School, and continues to do drawings whenever the mood strikes him.

Whittier, California—Circa 1984

Drawings done in delicate line were once frowned upon in editorial cartooning, but as artist-attorney Jim Bensfield offers in evidence here, and proves, they can be just as effective as any other style, *as long as the ideas are good!*

The GOP's White Elephant

A Bensfield GOP elephant. The editorial cartoonist gave it Richard Nixon's forelock, so there'd be no doubt as to who was "putting his foot in it."

The former chief counsel to the President tries his hand at (White) house painting, with disastrous results for both.

Charles O. Bissell, of Nashville, Tennessee, an editorial cartoonist for over 30 years, inherited his job at the *Tennessean* from Tom Little. He says, "It has been a very rewarding experience for me to know that any day I might be involved in a passionate cartoon slugfest."

In addition to providing drawings of a political nature Bissell does a weekly feature for his paper, called, *Bissell's Brave New World,* in which he was happy to take on "the polluters, the greedy, the wasters, the slothful, the synthesizers, the over-extenders, and just about everybody dedicated to making the world the mess it is today."

"Oh yes, when DDT killed off all the birds we achieved a new breakthrough in insect control."

"The Gallup poll says most women prefer Miss or Mrs. but we queen bees much prefer the new Mz-z-z-z-z-z."

An echo of the famous Scopes trial of the 1920's, when a Tennessee schoolteacher was found guilty of explaining to his pupils that man descended from the apes. That tree trunk was a lot thinner in those days!

As war flared up again in the Middle East, the editorial cartoonist heard wheels turning, like something was being turned off, and, as his fuel-less readers could later attest, he was right!

THE TUNNEL AT THE END OF THE LIGHT?
APRIL 10, 1973

Hawks on the war in Indochina couldn't possibly find any comfort in this Bissell cartoon, done in an appropriately somber mood.

"Controversy is what editorial cartooning is all about," says Charles Bissell, and adds, "James Branch Cabell, America's most profound and, of course, most forgotten satirist, once contended that life emulates art, rather than the other way around as some might suppose. As a cartoonist, I have always believed that this might just possibly be true."

Jerry Bittle, who majored in art in Wichita State University, first saw the light of day in Heber Springs, Arkansas, and always aspired to be a cartoonist, but he didn't think he could ever make a living at it. Hence, his earlier ambitions included being either a pharmacist or an architect.

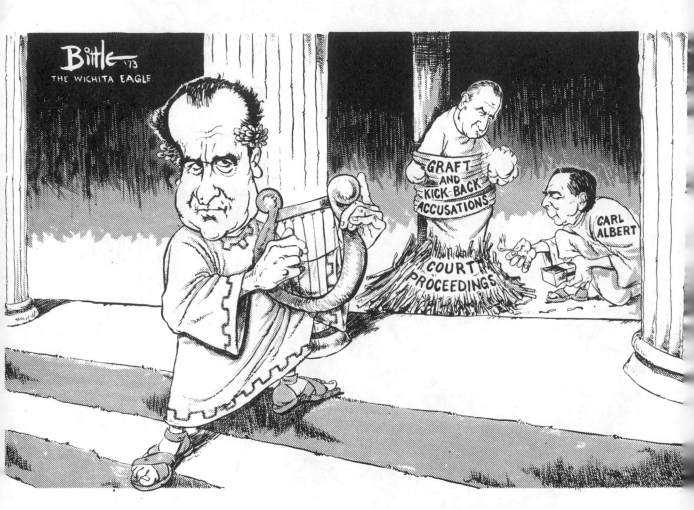

However, flunking math and science at school caused Bittle to change his mind about those other professions, a decision he has never regretted since discovering the tremendous opportunity for self-expression that editorial cartooning gives him.

Bittle describes his working arrangement with the paper—the Wichita *Eagle* and *Beacon*—this way: "Usually we have editorial meetings daily and discuss an event they want me to cartoon. Thus I sometimes don't see the actual editorial until it appears in print the next day."

"Not bad, Dick, but I can still see your lips moving."

Bittle took us to the office of a theatrical entrepreneur, as a Chief Executive whose act was faltering got ready to break in a new partner.

This was a fervent plea for the environment by the editorial cartoonist.

"Can you dig any faster, Al? The lights are a little dim in New Jersey."

"PEACE KEEPING DECISION A DIPLOMATIC VICTORY," stated the headline on the editorial page of the Sunday combined *Eagle and Beacon*, Oct. 28, 1973. The editorial continues:

"The United States appears to have won an important diplomatic victory in the United Nations. The Security Council voted unanimously Thursday to police the Middle East ceasefire with a U.N. emergency force that would exclude troops from the nuclear powers.

"If the temporary peace may be kept, the world may now proceed with the negotiations toward settlement that could bring lasting peace to the Middle East. It will be a long process, for the animosities are ancient and the differences deep.

"For the moment, the important thing is that the fighting has ceased, holocaust seems no longer imminent, and the United Nations has once again been demonstrated to be an extremely useful instrument for the settlement of dangerous disputes."

This is how Bittle illustrated the above editorial.

The still-smoking cannons, the terrified "observer" with shaking knees, the badly mangled dove of peace—all indicate that the editorial *cartoonist* might have been less optimistic at this point in time than the editorial *writer*.

"I guess readers must look at my work, because I do get my share of hate mail. This doesn't bother me too much. I just add them to my collection and go on about my business, hoping that at least part of the time I'm doing some good in the affairs of men," says Jerry Bittle.

Herbert Lawrence Block, known to the world as "Herblock," was born in Chicago, Illinois, and educated at Lake Forest College, Rutgers University, and the Art Institute of Chicago.

A two-time winner of the Pulitzer Prize, he began doing editorial cartoons for the Chicago *Daily News* during the Depression, later served in the armed forces when the Hitler shadow was spreading across Europe, and in 1946 returned to his profession, this time with the Washington *Post*.

Fifty-Star General

More than a half-dozen collections of Herblock's work have been published and, in addition to his Pulitzers, he has won awards from such organizations as the National Cartoonists Society, the Newspaper Guild, and the Capitol Press Club. In 1966 he designed a United States Postage Stamp commemorating the 175th anniversary of the Bill of Rights.

Showing his gift for inventiveness, the editorial cartoonist "sees" the face of Chairman Mao in this nuclear explosion set off by China.

Mushrooming Cloud

The shooting down of college students in 1970 by police and national guards in Kent, Ohio, and Jackson, Mississippi, was memorialized by Herblock in this sombre cartoon.

End Of School

Morrie Brickman, son of a Chicago shoe repairman, tried his hand at several different comic strips and panels before coming up with this one which, for obvious reasons, appears mostly on editorial pages rather than any other section of newspapers.

A Purple Heart veteran of the rugged Italian campaign during World War II, Morrie received his art training at the Art Institute in Chicago, and the Art Students League in New York City.

the small society  by Brickman

the small society by Brickman

the small society by Brickman

Brickman's pen line, seemingly careless and "thrown away," cleverly captures a bit of the twentieth-century chaos many readers occasionally feel in their lives, the unorthodox style of drawing dutifully complementing his "mad" ideas.

the small society   by Brickman

HOO-BOY! BY THE TIME WE GET OLD ENOUGH NOT TO CARE WHAT ANYBODY SAYS ABOUT US...

NOBODY SAYS ANYTHING—

ington Star Syndicate, Inc.   3-7   BRICKMAN

the small society   by Brickman

NEW ECONOMY COMPACT

I CAN PROMISE DELIVERY IN SIXTY DAYS—

BUT I'LL TELL YOU RIGHT NOW YOU WON'T GET IT—

ngton Star Syndicate, Inc.   3-8   BRICKMAN

the small society   by Brickman

I LIKE HIS SOFT SELL—

gton Star Syndicate, Inc.   3-9   BRICKMAN

Hubert J. Bushey, who was born in St. Albans, Vermont, had three suggestions offered him as a youngster: his mother wanted him to be a landscape painter, his father wanted him to be a railroad man like himself, and an uncle had the idea his nephew should enter the prize ring. Dutifully, Hubert tried them all, then graduated from the Boston Institute of Art and became an editorial cartoonist!

He is fondest of local or state issues, and works in a studio, rather than at the paper.

A tiff over the proposed banning of bottle tops, during which one of the adversaries said, "The government better get off our backs," gave Bushey this idea for a cartoon and a chance to draw a bucking bronco.

Frequently, this editorial cartoonist draws a "semi-realistic head on a smaller cartoon body," in the style used by Fitzpatrick and other caricaturists of the 1920's, as he has done here with a governor of Vermont.

Does Bushey feel that his style might change eventually? "I doubt it," he says, "although right now I'm experimenting with making more comic heads."

Hubert Bushey draws on Grumbacher's Glarco board-dot, using Windsor & Newton series 8- # 1-2-3 brushes, Gilliot #170-290 and 850 pens, and Kohinoor flexicolor #60 black crayons.

THE BURLINGTON
FREE PRESS —

Bob Chambers, Nova Scotia-born, went to New York at 19, and did animated cartoons for films and illustrated sheet music while studying nights at the Art Students League. In 1937, he joined the Halifax *Herald* and did editorial cartoons every day but Sunday.

Chambers has an honorary degree in law, from St. Francis Xavier University, at Antigonish, Nova Scotia, and has won the National Newspaper Award (the Canadian equivalent of the Pulitzer Prize) twice. "I'm not one of those go-for-the-jugular cartoonists," he says, and after years working in a "rather plush office" at the newspaper plant, has just started doing his work at home.

"You're pampering yourself – get up on your feet and jog around this great land of opportunity."

The Prime Minister of Canada delivered a doleful report on the state of affairs in this cartoon, and Chambers made him appropriately doleful.

No snakes in Ireland? The editorial cartoonist showed a few here.

Modern Saint Patrick — modern approach

This news break from Ireland possibly seemed funny at the time, and indeed it might have been if the fighting only ceased!

Bob Chambers' cartoons are 10 X 12 inches, approximately one third larger than they appear when reproduced. They are drawn on two-ply kid finish Strathmore board, using a 170 Gilliot pen nib, and occasionally a #3 Windsor and Newton watercolor brush. Format Ben Day screen No. 7015 covering large middletone areas, completes his pictures.

"Come out with your hands in the air — but don't hurry — I'm being paid time and a half."

Above, Chambers obviously had a good time burlesquing the Royal Canadian Northwest Mounties.

Paul Conrad graduated from the University of Iowa in 1950, and for 13 years thereafter he was employed as editorial cartoonist by the Denver *Post*.

Later, occupying the position of editorial cartoonist with the Los Angeles *Times*, Conrad won two Pulitzer Prizes, (1964 and 1971); three National Sigma Delta Chi Awards (1963, 1969, and 1971); and the Overseas Press Club Award (1970). He is one member of the profession who insists on absolute independence in his work and, thankfully, his paper respected that position.

Two views of the 37th President of the United States, by Paul Conrad: first as an entomologist might have seen him, featuring a web even a spider can't spin—

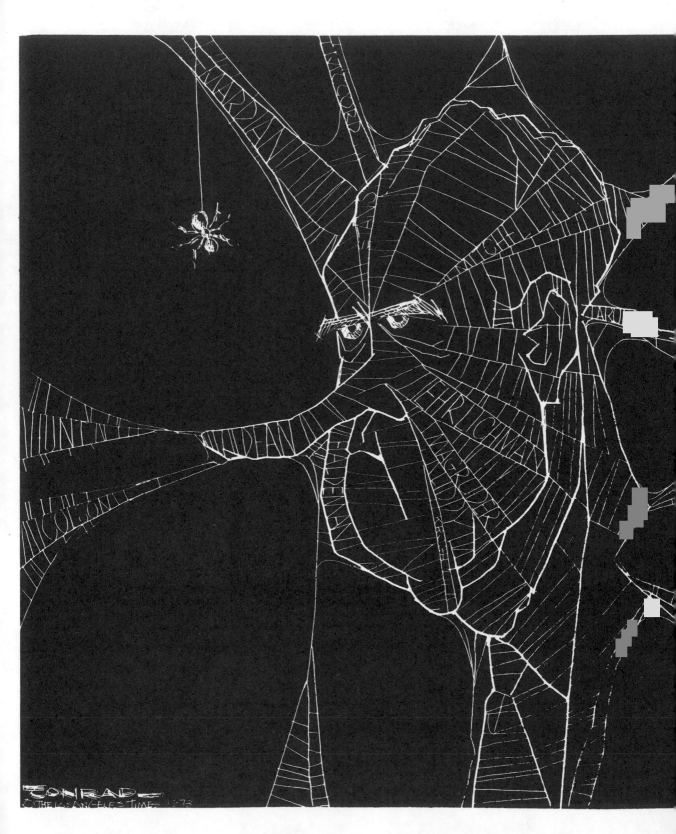

—and now the same Chief Executive as William Shakespeare might have conjured him, with the editorial cartoonist skillfully capturing some of the uneasiness of the head that wore a crown.

O THAT I WERE AS GREAT AS MY GRIEF, OR LESSER THAN MY NAME!
OR THAT I COULD FORGET WHAT I HAVE BEEN!
OR NOT REMEMBER WHAT I MUST BE NOW!
KING RICHARD II. ACT III, SCENE III

Eugene Craig, of Fort Wayne, Indiana, did his first political cartoon at the age of 18, joining the *News-Sentinel* in his native city immediately after graduating from high school. Craig later worked for the Brooklyn *Eagle* until that paper folded, then went to the Columbus *Dispatch*, where in addition to his regular chores for the editorial page, he drew a comic feature, *Forever Female*.

In 1951, Craig designed a U.S. postage stamp, "The Battle of Brooklyn." The Freedom Foundation in Valley Forge has awarded him its top cartoon award three times.

YEAR OF THE TIGER?

OLE!

MASS TRANSIT PROBLEM

CONGRESS

This bull of Craig's was beefed up only to suggest he'd be around for a long, long time, in spite of what any matadors thought about it.

TWO ENDS OF A COW

COST OF CLEARING SUEZ CANAL

SOVIET INDIAN OCEAN USE OF SUEZ CANAL

Uncle Sam takes care of a Craig cow on one end, while the USSR handles the "udder." (That's not milk Farmer Leonid Brezhnev is after, anyway.)

Getting an okayed rough from his editor, Eugene Craig uses a light box to trace his drawing onto a Bead Repco board twice the size of the printed cartoon. Starting with a No. 4 Windsor Newton brush, he rapidly lays in the major elements, then uses Esterbrook Probate pens for lettering and the Hunt bowl-point pen for detail. Bradley broadlyne crayon and Blaisdell china-marke for grays, and Q-white for touch-ups complete the picture.

Gib Crockett, of the Washington *Star*, was born in the nation's capital and educated there, as well as in Kingsport, Tennessee.

A former sports cartoonist, art director, and free-lance illustrator, Crockett's hobbies include wood carving and landscape painting. His work has been standouts in many exhibitions.

'ISN'T IT TIME YOU BROKE THAT UP?'

An editorial cartoonist must constantly look for symbols in his work, and here an ordinary shopping cart seemed to suggest an inescapable entrapment to Crockett, as he contemplated the plight of a housewife faced with the ever-rising cost of living.

'GET ME OUT OF HERE!'

'WHEE!'

What do we have here? Why, it's a Chief Executive bathing in the cesspool of his administration, as his successor Gerald Ford, an avowed swimmer, is en route to take the plunge himself, blithely ignoring all that flotsam and jetsam.

As we can see, Gib Crockett thinks out his ideas carefully, making each one an editorial in itself and fun for newspaper readers and the whole family to study.

Tom Curtis, who has become known from coast to coast as probably the leading cartoonist-spokesman for the conservative point of view, was born in New York City just prior to the Depression. He received a degree in architecture from Harvard University, where he was cartoonist for the *Harvard Lampoon* for three years.

After service in the Army, Curtis turned to free-lance cartooning in 1966 and became a regular contributor to the *National Review, Roll Call,* the *New Guard,* and *Triumph.*

He became staff editorial cartoonist for the Milwaukee *Sentinel* in August, 1969, and has won three George Washington Honor Medal awards from Freedom Foundation at Valley Forge.

"I place great faith in the freedom of the individual as a key to happiness and productivity. But I feel little freedom can exist where there is no law and order. Therefore, I oppose anarchy and believe that unjust laws should be changed through the accepted channels of the legislature rather than breaking those laws to force a confrontation," says Curtis.

"For the time being, try some aspirin."

"Do I smell blood?"

A killer shark (beautifully drawn) was used here to illustrate the theory that the impeachment of an American President would be of benefit to certain enemy nations.

The rat, that ancient symbol of everything loathesome (again drawn excellently), represents a common enemy to all mankind, in the above.

Three more cartoons by Curtis showing—

—the voracious appetite it takes to run a federal health plan—

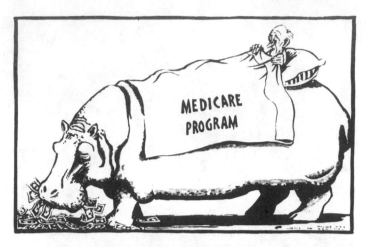

Extravagant accommodations

—what we might come to if more funds weren't provided for our sea power—

"Somebody bring some paste!"

—and, finally, a putdown for a certain "liberal" TV news commentator.

"We can destroy our credibility without your help, Mr. Agnew!"

Craig Curtiss, whose work has been appearing in the Billings (Montana) *Gazette* since the late 1960's, became fascinated with editorial cartooning while he was still a lad in high school.

His education, professionally, has consisted mainly of studying the theories, techniques, and ideas of other cartoonists right from the newspapers and magazines in which they appear.

"HI, HO !"

NEW COP ON THE BEAT

Three editorial cartoons by Curtiss, about three different topics.

One, a preoccupation with the "Red Menace" (Students for a Democratic Society), on the part of two outstanding citizens.

FREE, BLACK AND THIRTY—NINE.

U.S. ATTY. GEN. = *HEY,* J. ED
FBI DIRECTOR = YES, JOHN ?
U.S. ATTY. GEN. = WHAT'S BLACK AND WHITE
AND RED ALL OVER ?
FBI DIRECTOR = THE *SDS!*

Two, a memorial drawing for a slain black leader, done simply, yet with great dignity.

Three, a conception of "Hollywood mobster" Leonid Brezhnev about to dump the President of Czechoslovakia (into a river, presumably).

Craig. Curtiss doesn't bother showing his editors rough sketches of his ideas. Instead, he proceeds directly with a finished drawing, using coquille paper, good sable brushes, and extra dense india ink.

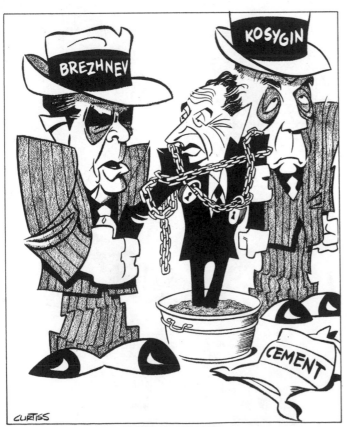

IS TAKING COMRADE
DUBCEK *SURFING..*

Charlie Daniel, an ex-Marine, majored in political science at the University of North Carolina. From grade school on, he longed to become a professional cartoonist, but unfortunately received only rejection slips for the work he submitted to various publications.

In 1958, however, Charlie landed in Knoxville as an editorial cartoonist and stayed at that post, doing six drawings a week. "My love for comic strips and gag cartoons may be seen in my style, I hope," he says.

The editorial cartoonist ventures to show what things may yet come to, and, funny or not, his work becomes a criticism of the economy.

The familiar face of a Secretary of State suddenly injected into the cast of characters removes all suspicion that this is "escapist" humor.

Charlie Daniel's cartoons are as thought-provoking as if they had been done in a far more serious vein and, as much as any member of his profession, he is a social satirist.

Jim Dobbins, who has received many awards for his work, started drawi[ng]
six cartoons a week in 1952 and has been at it ever since, going from t[he]
Lowell (Massachusetts) *Sun,* to the New York *Daily News,* to the n[ow]
defunct Boston *Post,* and eventually landing with the Boston *Hera[ld]
Traveler.*

A Navy flyer during World War II, stationed in the South Pacific,
Dobbins, a former teacher of art and English in the Boston school system,
received the Air Medal and Distinguished Flying Cross. He was educated
at the Massachusetts College of Art and Boston University Graduate
School of Education, and has ten children.

TO THE VICTOR GO THE SPOILS

Tolerance is the theme here, as editorial cartoonist Jim Dobbins asked his readers to look deep into their own hearts and help remove the monster that seems to be stalking the nation

WHAT OUR FRIENDLY DEMOCRATIC SYSTEM HAS BECOM

Jim Dobbins goes to the office several times a week, does one or two cartoons a day to fit the six-a-week schedule. He no longer does roughs, simply mentions to his editors the subjects he has chosen. If there is a "problem," they caution him. "I live within a broad editorial policy, but that doesn't mean I can always do what I want," he says. "Perhaps two or three times a year a cartoon is killed. I keep a few drawings in reserve, in case such a thing happens."

Tom Engelhardt was born in St. Louis, Missouri, and grew up there studying the great Daniel R. Fitzpatrick cartoons in the *Post-Dispatch*.

After a stint in the Air Force during the Korean War, Tom continued his art studies at Oxford University, England. During his two years there, he frequently took "pack-on-back" tours of the Continent, then returned to the States and the School of Visual Arts in New York City.

'JUST GIVE US THE TOOLS AND WE'LL GET THE JOB DONE'

Thurs., July 6, 1967   ST. LOUIS POST-DISPATCH

In 1962, after a long period doing free-lance work and a year of editorial cartooning with Newspaper Enterprise Association, he applied for the job at his old hometown newspaper and was accepted.

Engelhardt says he is seldom satisfied with his finished product, always vowing to do better the next day. Once when he mentioned this to Fitzpatrick, the retired cartoonist assured him that if he ever got to the point where he was satisfied with his work, he'd be a failure—counsel Tom has never forgotten.

This cartoon, says Engelhardt, "shows us how President Nixon, steering school busing by the erratic map of political expediency, not only set back the painful gains made toward educational equality, but also undermined the judicial system by attempting to restrict courts' jurisdictions."

Hit-And-Run Driver

Day and night it was bargain time at the White House—for Big Business, that is, as we can see by examining those limousines pulling up to the front door and, in particular, the cigar-smoking gent in the rear seat of the one just coming into view.

Open For Business

Here Engelhardt ridicules phony patriotism as manifested by such absurdities as monogrammed aprons and bumper stickers.

'The Trouble With This Country Is Nobody Respects The Flag Anymore'

Were the American people satisfied with the spending plans proposed by the Nixon administration? The gargantuan figure on the left sharply signified Engelhardt's own dissatisfaction with budget priorities.

Once Tom Engelhardt (who formerly blackened in the squares in crossword puzzles for a living!) has worked out the idea for his daily cartoon, he proceeds with a finish, using Strathmore bristol board and doing his actual drawing 13 X 18 inches, a preliminary sketch having been laid in beforehand with a 4H pencil. India ink, Gilliot 303 pens, lithographic crayon, Prismacolor black pencils, brushes and white paint constitute the rest of the materials used by him.

Nuclear Giant And Humanitarian Midget

Lou "Eric" Erickson became editorial cartoonist for the Atlanta *Journal* in 1961, and as one of his bosses immediately noted, "Instead of the ax, he uses a needle. By showing the absurdity of so many situations, he weakens villains who never could have been hurt by the view-with-alarm approach."

'WELL IT'S BETTER THAN NOTHIN'!'

The son of a railroad engineer in Marcus, Washington, Lou volunteered for aerial gunnery, glider pilot, and paratrooper during World War II and, as fate would have it, wound up doing a comic strip for the *Army Times*.

'LET US TAKE HEART IN WHAT OUR PRESIDENT SAYS: IT IS NOT A CRISIS BUT ONLY A PROBLEM!'

If it weren't actually happening to them, too, during the fuel shortage, some of Erickson's readers might have thought this situation was really funny!

Another cartoon to make his readers laugh, if only it weren't so personal!

The tell-tale signs of the comic artist are easily apparent in the work of Lou Erickson, whose readers must enjoy having him give them "comedy" straight off the front page.

THE CENSOR WHO CAME TO DINNER AND STAYED AND STAYED AND STAYED

Jules Feiffer, a native New Yorker, studied at the Art Students League and Pratt Institute and began drawing for the *Village Voice* in 1956, eventually achieving syndication in the United States and abroad.

A regular contributor to *Playboy* and other publications, Feiffer won an Academy Award in 1961 for his animated cartoon, "Munro," about a five-year-old child accidentally drafted into the army. His books and novels include *Sick, Sick, Sick; Passionella and Other Stories; Harry the Rat with Women;* and *The Great Comic Book Heroes.* For the Broadway stage he has written *Little Murders* (winner of an Outer Circle Drama Critic's Award and voted best play of the year by London critics), *God Bless,* and *The White House Murder Case.* His *Carnal Knowledge,* one of the most controversial motion pictures in the history of the film industry, was the subject of a U.S. Supreme Court case.

Feiffer's total disregard for party lines is clearly evident in this 1972 cartoon in which three Presidents in succession pontificate almost exactly alike on the "end" of a war, then a fourth one carries on, ad infinitum. . . .

THE SOUTH VIETNAMESE HAVE MADE GREAT PROGRESS. THEY ARE NOW BEARING THE BRUNT OF THE BATTLE. AND WE CAN NOW SEE THE DAY..

WHEN NO MORE AMERICANS WILL BE INVOLVED THERE AT ALL. AND THAT IS WHY I SAY TO YOU TONIGHT..

LET US END THE WAR. BUT LET US END IT IN SUCH A WAY THAT THE YOUNGER BROTHERS AND SONS OF THE BRAVE MEN WHO HAVE FOUGHT..

© 1972 JULES FEIFFER 6-4

Dist. Publishers-Hall Syndicate

WILL NOT HAVE TO FIGHT AGAIN IN SOME OTHER VIETNAM AT SOME TIME IN THE FUTURE.

The ambiguity of politicians has always fascinated editorial cartoonists. Here, in primer style, Feiffer spotlighted the dual personality of Robert Kennedy at one point during his career in public office, which included the fight against organized crime while Attorney General.

The accurate likeness in these varied caricatures of one subject contributed to the success of this cartoon by Feiffer, who undoubtedly appreciated the late Senator's charisma as much as his most devoted admirers.

THESE ARE THE BOBBY TWINS. ONE IS A GOOD BOBBY. ONE IS A BAD BOBBY. 1.

THE GOOD BOBBY IS A COURAGEOUS REFORMER. THE BAD BOBBY MAKES DEALS. 2.

THE GOOD BOBBY SENT FEDERAL TROOPS DOWN SOUTH TO ENFORCE CIVIL RIGHTS. THE BAD BOBBY APPOINTED RACIST JUDGES DOWN SOUTH TO ENFORCE CIVIL RIGHTS. 3.

THE GOOD BOBBY IS A FERVENT CIVIL LIBERTARIAN. THE BAD BOBBY IS A FERVENT WIRE TAPPER. 4.

THE GOOD BOBBY IS ILL AT EASE WITH LIBERALS. THE BAD BOBBY IS ILL AT EASE WITH GROWNUPS. 5.

IF YOU WANT ONE BOBBY TO BE YOUR PRESIDENT YOU WILL HAVE TO TAKE BOTH... FOR BOBBIES ARE WIDELY NOTED FOR THEIR FAMILY UNITY. 6.

In this cartoon we immediately see that Feiffer's "King Kong" bears a startling resemblance to a U.S. President. The fact that the creature has climbed to the top of the Capitol in Washington, D.C., rather than the Empire State Building in New York, doesn't make us any less certain of his identity.

4-28 ©1974 JULES FEIFFER

Aspiring editorial cartoonists should note the drawing of Kong, how fearsome though funny he is, the action of his body whether he's perched atop a national monument or moving up Pennsylvania Avenue, and above all, that *the satire here is directed against the reader himself!*

Satirizing his own profession, Feiffer reveals the trials and tribulations of an editorial cartoonist, or a day in the life of one trying to handle a very sensitive subject and please his editor at the same time.

Equally endowed as an artist and writer, Jules Feiffer's work was among the first to break the taboo traditional in American newspapers which forbade publishing drawings that contradicted the tone of editorial policies. His ideas obviously spring from a mind unwilling to compromise with half-truths and phoniness.

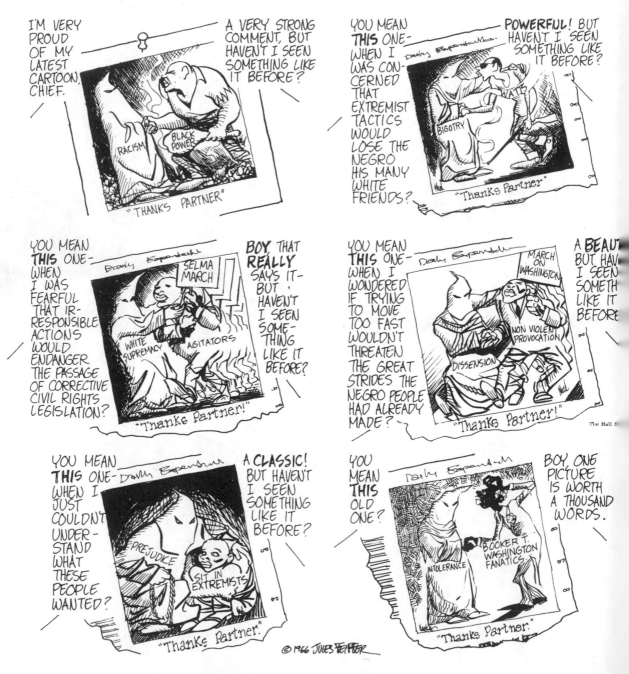

Jack H. Ficklen, a native of Waco, Texas, was nicknamed Herc at an early age, "due to the ease with which he destroyed sand castles." Starting at the Dallas *News* as a copy boy, he rose to the art department, doing layouts and photo-retouching, and finally landed on the editorial page, pinch-hitting for the regular staff cartoonist.

During World War II, Herc left his paper to serve in the armed

forces, participating in five campaigns in the European Theatre of action. He has received some fifty-odd prizes for his work, including a dozen Freedom Foundation Awards.

© Dallas News

"I'M NOT APATHETIC, I JUST DON'T GIVE A DAMN."

Were the scandals rocking both major political parties, causing some Americans to lose faith? Ficklen's "typical voter" (so upset over these, perhaps, that he forgot to slip on a robe) seems irked enough to do more than just feel that way.

Wondrous though our free elections, the editorial cartoonist reminds us that "garbage" will still be here the morning after, too.

ECOLOGIST

Perhaps weary of the day-to-day struggle he participates in with his work, and a bit fatalistic about it all, Herc Ficklen has now returned to his first love, painting, and has created many noteworthy portraits and landscapes.

Ed Fischer began his full-time career on the opinion page of the Minneapolis *Star* in 1966, after two and a half years with the Tulsa (Oklahoma) *Tribune*. He says he tried fashioning his style of drawing after Paul Conrad, whom he admires greatly.

Fischer, a product of Minneapolis, enjoys most doing editorial cartoons on local issues. "Being on the scene, it's a pleasure seeing my work

bring about a change in the social phenomena that always irked me, no matter how trivial," he says. "For this reason, I try to make certain that at least a few of the seven cartoons I do each week are local in substance."

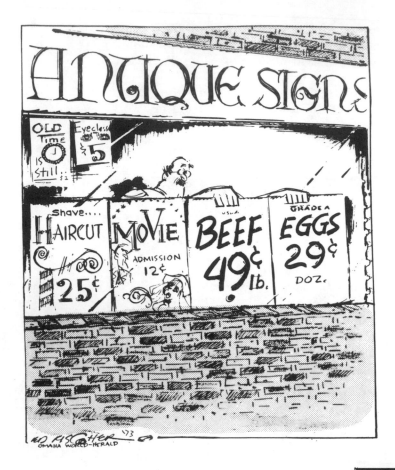

This nostalgic cartoon might have appeared in Ripley's *Believe It Or Not* by accident, though readers would probably not believe prices were ever *that* low!

The editorial cartoonist shows us, with deep affection, what the proposed "bait" might look like to an American boy of army age,

"For anyone who cares enough about society to consider entering this profession, I strongly recommend not only a good basic background in art, but as broad and general an education as well," says Ed Fischer.

Tom Flannery was born in Carbondale, Pennsylvania. He studied at the University of Scranton in his native state, and at Pratt Institute in New York.

He worked as an accountant for hotels in New York City, and as a bouncer in a theater in the Greenpoint section of Brooklyn. Flannery

served with the Army Air Force during World War II, earning a Bronze Star. He also contributed drawings to *Yank*, the U.S. Army publication.

Prior to his affiliation in Baltimore, he did editorial cartoons for the Lowell (Massachusetts) *Sun*.

If the winter of 1973 wasn't a miserable one, it certainly felt that way to many Americans, what with the oil pinch and other vital shortages. Small wonder, then, that the horn of plenty seemed little more than a hollow shell to Flannery at the time.

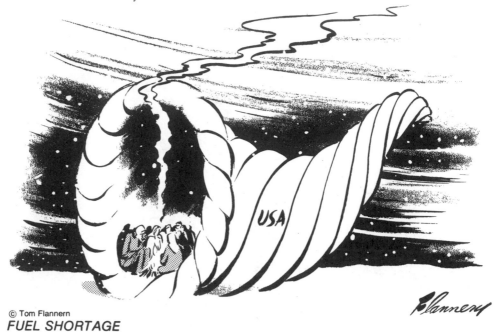

© Tom Flannern
FUEL SHORTAGE

Drawn in this editorial cartoonist's usual lucid style, the ship of state appeared headed for Davy Jones's locker as the Captain—er, President—steadfastly continued announcing his "price controls."

P.S. to add to the confusion, Tom Flannery's ship of state resembled a speedboat!

© Tom Flannern
"NOW HEAR THIS—WE'RE GOING TO HAVE A LIFEBOAT DRILL"

Dan Gibson, editorial cartoonist for the *Rocky Mountain News,* was born in Appleton, Wisconsin, but grew up in Indiana and Illinois. After serving in the Navy, he worked as a sign painter while attending night classes at the Chicago Art Institute. Subsequently, he also studied drawing at Ventura Junior College, in California, and at the University of Denver, in Colorado.

Gibson's cartoons frequently focus on such topics as the energy crisis and how they affect tourism in his adopted state.

I'LL SEE WHAT I CAN DO FOR YOU, BACK IN WASHINGTON

The grim prospect of a world sporting event being held outside of Colorado, after the state's voters turned thumbs down on spending more money for the event, inspired this "Frankenstein" drawing, done in pen and ink, with screens for shading. Underneath that gravestone rests the Denver Olympic Organizing Committee.

NEVER SAY DIE

In the cartoon below the title is brief, the picture doesn't even have a figure, yet it conveys to the reader a most poignant story, complete in every detail, of a nation conceivably on the way to destroying itself.

Dan Gibson uses a #3 Windsor-Newton red sable brush, an inflexible Esterbrook #322 pen, and 3-ply illustration boards, sometimes crafttint paper. His lettering is done with speed-ball pens.

TARGET DEMOCRACY

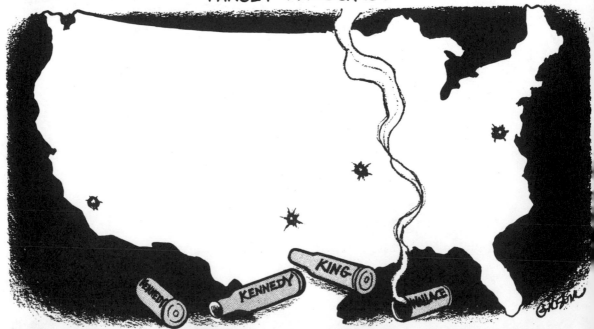

Louis Payne Goodwin inherited the nickname Doc from his father who was a medical practitioner in Lincoln County, Tennessee. A Navy parachute rigger during World War II, Doc graduated from the University of Tennessee in 1948 with a B.A. in English.

Like Gene Craig, his co-worker on the Columbus *Dispatch*, he does a comic feature for the paper, entitled *Mostly Male*, corresponding somewhat with Craig's *Forever Female*.

A former copy boy on a Spokane (Washington) paper, Goodwin says, "My first published cartoon came at the age of 14 when I won an award of three dollars. Immediately, I knew where the money was at."

"IT'S BEING RECALLED BY THE FACTORY!"

TAIL OF THE KITE

The question automatically raised in readers' minds by this amusing drawing: How high would that kite go?

HIS BITE IS WORSE THAN HIS BARK.

Man's best friend had to be big and fierce here, and not too friendly, according to the editorial cartoonist.

Thus, Doc Goodwin's diagnosis of an ailing society, in part!

Hugh Haynie, educated at public schools and the College of William and Mary in his native state, Virginia, and at the University of Louisville in Kentucky, was affiliated with the Richmond (Virginia) *Times-Dispatch*, the Greensboro (North Carolina) *Daily News*, and the Atlanta *Journal*, before joining the Louisville *Courier-Journal* in 1958.

"I'm O.K. You're O.K."

Serving with the Coast Guard, 1944-1946, and 1951-1952, Haynie, a member of the Phi Beta Kappa and Omicron Delta Kappa societies, was named one of the Ten Outstanding Young Men of the Nation by the U.S. Junior Chamber of Commerce in 1962. He has received many awards for his work.

© 1973 The Courier-Journal

"So I'm an odd-looking Arab, am I? Well, I must say, you certainly don't look Jewish!"

The editorial cartoonist offered us a snatch of strange dialogue during the Middle East conflict, uttered by some rather strange-looking specimens from the Wild Kingdom.

Here's Haynie being funny with a nursery rhyme (although it was hurting readers in the breadbasket!)

Now, Sammy the Baker had oodles of grain, Till he sold it abroad for capital gain...

WHEAT $HORTAGE $PECIAL

Thus, sing for your sup you pitiful oaf, To the tune of about a dollar a loaf!

© 1974 The Courier-Journal

Expecting a fair shake? Here's the hand to expect it from, warned editorial cartoonist Hanie.

Hugh Haynie does six drawings a week and his work is syndicated in 43 newspapers from coast to coast. His originals are 14 X 19 inches.

DISTRIBUTED BY L. A. TIMES SYNDICATE

© 1973 The Courier-Journal

"Okay, long-green giant! You're getting smaller . . . ever smaller . . . ever smaller . . . ever smaller . . ."

Draper Hill, Boston-born and educated at Harvard, and at the Slade School of Fine Arts in London, saw his first political cartoon appear in the *Harvard Times-Republican* and the *Harvard Lampoon* in the mid-1950's. After college, he worked as writer, cartoonist, and illustrator for the Quincy (Massachusetts) *Patriot Ledger*.

A London resident for much of the early 1960's, Hill catalogued and helped organize one of the largest international exhibitions of historical cartoons and caricatures ever held, at the request of the Arts Council of Great Britain.

In his own drawings for the Memphis *Commercial Appeal*, Hill, who is the author of numerous biographies and studies of early pictorial satire, tries to vary his approach, to avoid predictability. He compares an editorial cartoon to the carved figurehead at the prow of a ship, in relation to the newspaper in which it appears.

Playmate of the Year

© The Commercial Appeal

You've Come A Long Way, Baby!

July 4, 1973, and Draper Hill takes a hard look at Miss Liberty up to her hips in pollution, but still holding that torch of freedom high.

A harried President Nixon did some tall explaining, and the editorial cartoonist obligingly trotted out the militia for him.

Here the editorial cartoonist turned his attention to different matters including the report of a young, out-of-town trollop infiltrating the local police department.

A "fifth column" in the Memphis police force.

Inflation.

Tally-Ho!

The Endless Summer

Foreign affairs.

Here Hill takes us into a pool hall for a view of Palestine guerrilla leader Arafat "calling a shot."

'Eight ball in the corner pocket'

A Vice-President's tragic descent into disgrace, if not oblivion, was captured with consummate skill in this cartoon by Hill, who describes his job as "hitting responsibility below the belt."

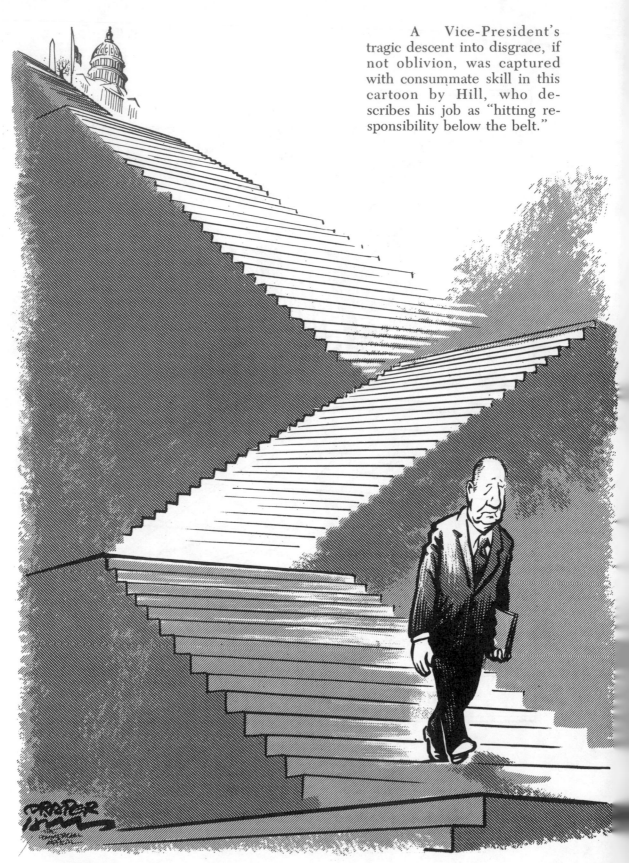

In this Hill cartoon, President Gerald Ford wrestles a snake whose features are unmistakenly those of former President Nixon.

Draper Hill's principal weapon is a "juicy number four red sable brush, used on prepared drawing paper that permits the chemical application of two gray tones." After one or two very rough sketches, he develops the final version directly on the prepared paper with a 6H pencil, working about one-third larger than the final reproduction.

"You've got to admit we're getting Watergate behind us."

C.P. Houston, of Covington, Tennessee, is a former army sergeant, ad writer, insurance representative, lumber-mill hand, department-store clerk, hobo, bouncer, hotel clerk, and medical-records inspector.

Calling on the *Chronicle* editor one day in the middle 1960's to inquire about the easiest way to become an editorial cartoonist, he not only got the advice, but the job.

Houston's cartoons are now syndicated in over a hundred daily papers.

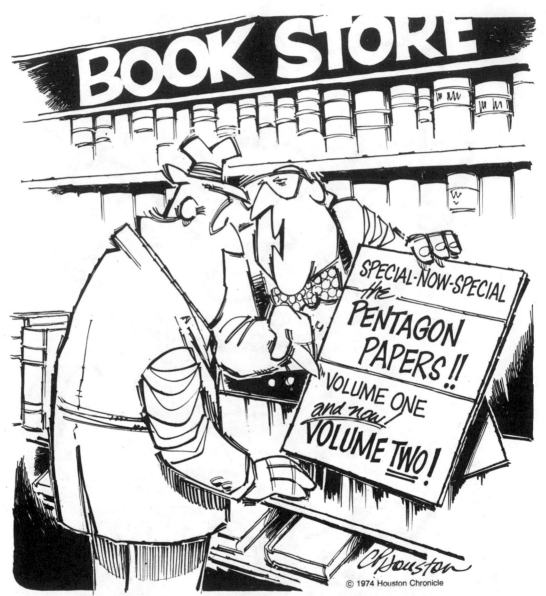

"Volume one being those swiped FROM them; volume two being those swiped BY them!"

Working within a comic strip format, Houston, in these four samples of his brand of satire, hands us a chuckle over X-rated movies, the Playboy culture, the State of the Union, and a very touchy political issue—

Karl Hubenthal, a Marine Corps veteran during World War II, became an editorial cartoonist for the Hearst newspapers in 1935, and with the Los Angeles *Herald-Examiner* specifically in 1935. A former sports cartoonist, his work has been displayed almost everywhere in the world, from the White House in Washington, D.C., to the National Portrait Gallery in London, England. He has been nominated six times for the National Cartoonists Society's coveted "Reuben" (the profession's "Oscar") and won 21 Freedom Foundation Medals, in addition to numerous other awards.

HIS OWN WORST ENEMY

© L.A. Herald-Examiner

Working at home, rather than in the city room, Hubie's day usually consists of approximately four hours "rough and think time," and two hours for the finish. "I have long since passed the stage where I need to show my editor a rough. I still do them, however, for my own discipline and find that quite often a second look will develop an idea better than the first." He has complete freedom on ideas as well as policy, and his only obligation is to "fill that 3-column hole each day."

DAMASCUS BLADE

SIAMESE TWIN

THE EXORCIST

A former sports cartoonist could hardly be expected to let a great moment in the national pastime go by unnoticed. Here we see Babe Ruth looking down from the heavens as he and Henry Aaron, holder of a new record for home runs, share the same baseball hat.

The paper Karl Hubenthal prefers is made by Grumbacher and designated as Rough Stipple. "I use Windsor Newton, series 7, sable brushes and Catalina white, one that was developed for Disney Studios to use on their cello-frames," he says.

Etta Hulme, one of the few ladies in the world ever to practice editorial cartooning, began by drawing on paper bags in her family's grocery store at an early age. After graduating from the University of Texas, she held various positions in the commercial art field, including a two-year stint with the Disney Studios in Burbank, California, as an animator.

"IN TWENTY FIVE WORDS OR LESS,
THAT IDEA WON HIM A TRIP ABROAD"

Married to a former Army captain, once stationed in Germany, she persuaded the Fort Worth *Star-Telegram* to start publishing three of her cartoons a week in 1971.

"WELL, HE'S EASIER TO CONTROL THAN MARTHA!"

FBI

JOHN MITCHELL

ETTA HULME

Fort Worth STAR-TELEGRAM

Above, a bloodhound symbolizes the misuse of a federal agency in relation to the marriage of a former Attorney General.

This cartoon lampooned an effort to bolster the testimony of a Presidential secretary regarding tapings monitored by her in the White House.

"OUR TAPE EXPERT HERE IS PREPARED TO DEMONSTRATE THAT THE ERASURE MARKS MAY NOT HAVE BEEN MADE MANUALLY"

UHER 5000

WHITE HOUSE

ETTA HULME

"I'LL TELL YOU WHAT—YOU DEFINE AN IMPEACHABLE OFFENSE, AND THEN I'LL DEFINE EXECUTIVE PRIVILEGE"

The ultra-bored expression on the judge's face gave this cartoon the precise satirical effect Hulme wanted to achieve here.

On a different tack, we get a tip on the stock market from the editorial cartoonist, *maybe*.

Etta Hulme's cartoon style, bright and gay, witty and devastating, represents a giant step towards unisex in the profession, if other ladies will only follow her.

"GOLD AND SILVER ARE GOING GREAT—BUT FOR A REALLY SOLID INVESTMENT, MAY WE SUGGEST HANK AARON BUBBLEGUM CARDS?"

Cy Hungerford, of the Pittsburgh *Post-Gazette*, in his seventh decade as an editorial cartoonist, is certainly the undisputed dean of his profession. The Pittsburgh *Sun* (now defunct) sent him abroad in 1924 to bring back his impressions of Europe and North Africa; in 1937 he returned to Europe to cover the coronation of King George VI; and in 1953 he was present at the wedding of Mrs. Wallace Simpson and the Duke of Windsor.

Covering many national political conventions, starting with the Republican Party nomination of Warren G. Harding in Chicago in 1920, Hungerford claims he has never had an editor give him "trouble."

The Nudity Crisis

The nostalgia offered by this remarkable artist engenders trust and confidence; the "easy" style camouflages a most extensive knowledge of drawing.

A Happy Dream

Uncle Sam Finally Got a Lift

Down through the years with Cy Hungerford we meet such people as William Jennings Bryan, the celebrated silver-tongued orator; Russia's Joseph Stalin; John L. Lewis of the United Mine Worker's union; and U.S. Presidents Truman, Eisenhower, Kennedy, Johnson, and Nixon—all drawn with the same dash and aplomb the editorial cartoonist had when he began.

Seeking Information   By Hungerford

September 21, 1903

eyebrows vs. Mustaches   By Hungerford

Jan. 8, 1952

Sept. 22, 1952

March 15, 1948   Leap Year   By Hungerford   September Morn   By

The One-Man Band   By Hungerford   In Step   By Hungerford   March Came In Like A Lamb   By

March 2, 1962   Oct. 11, 1965   March 2, 1973

Jim Ivey, formerly of the San Francisco *Examiner,* became editorial cartoonist for the *Sentinel-Star,* in Orlando, Florida, in 1970.

Fondest of caricature, and the captionless drawing, Ivey is curator of the Cartoon Museum in Orlando, and a director of the San Francisco Academy of Comic Art. He has written extensively on all facets of the profession.

Does that unkind caricature indicate a disrespect for the Speaker of the House? Not necessarily. Jim Ivey might simply have had difficulty getting a likeness. An ancient proverb says, "Hell hath no fury like a woman scorned, or a caricaturist with a subject hard to capture."

"WHAT, ME WORRY?"

IVEY

© 1974 Sentinel Star

Here we have the 37th President of the United States in the center of a family portrait, having a whiff of Havana cigar smoke deliberately wafted his way by the Premier of Cuba, with likenesses of all those involved neatly captured by the editorial cartoonist.

With an economy of line, Ivey ventures to suggest what happened to a mysterious $100,000 "contribution" billionaire Howard Hughes gave the Committee to Reelect the President (Nixon), and intimates that sooner or later we may all be following it down the same place.

IVEY

© 1973 Sentinel Star

... AND HERE COMES THE KITCHEN SINK !!

Pen and ink sketches by Ivey, show a native American product turning up in Moscow's Red Square, of all places (on May Day, yet!).

IVEY

Cecil Jensen, born in Ogden, Utah, attended the Chicago Academy of Fine Arts and got an editorial page position with the *Daily News* in that city, following a brief stint doing political cartoons for a now defunct Los Angeles newspaper.

Creator of the once highly successful comic strip, "Elmo," Jensen has won awards from Sigma Delta Chi, the National Safety Council, and other organizations.

"Oh, where are the skies not cloudy all day?"

© Chicago Daily News

Jensen provides us with a view, from the 50-yard line, of the struggle going on between two opposing sides in a recent administration.

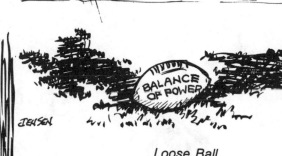

Loose Ball
© Chicago Daily News

A thoroughly repentant elephant here, who is probably wondering if he can turn over a new leaf, or if that whole darn book got wet.

"Your place in my book is assured"
© 1973 Chicago Daily News

Cecil Jensen does his drawings with a crow quill pen and india ink, on boards 12 X 18 inches in size; and he does them now from the Ozark mountains, where he is semiretired but still "doing a few a week to keep from getting senile."

Yardley Jones, "a maverick Welshman" according to his own description, was born in Liverpool, England, and educated there and in Wales, where he studied architecture and worked in construction while trying to eke out a living doing gag cartoons for magazines. Moving to Canada, finally, with "his wife and rejection slips," he designed greeting cards, painted signs on gas station windows, and eventually broke into editorial cartooning by bombarding the editor of the Edmonton (Alberta) *Journal* with rough sketches every morning.

"Finally you two have something in common — a hangover . . ."

Seven years later, Jones moved his talents over to the now-defunct Toronto *Telegram*, then, finally went to work for the Montreal *Star*.

Another problem, with the Red Man, this time in Canada, and with no need for John Wayne to come ridin' up from Hollywood and interfere.

"Some gentlemen here, Prime Minister — say they've come to collect the rent . . ."

Jack Jurden, who has won awards from the Freedom Foundation and the Delaware, Maryland Press Association, entered the military service in 1944 after graduation from high school and served in the South Pacific. Afterwards he worked as a photoengraver, doing free-lance drawing on the side.

In 1962 he began full-time editorial cartooning for the Wilmington Delaware *Evening Journal.*

A less irked-looking fisherman behind that snarled line might not have been so amusing here.

A thousand words on pollution couldn't have been as effective as this one single cartoon by Jack Jurden.

And to make things worse the waters polluted

Jon Kennedy was born in Springfield, Missouri, attended schools in his native city, and got his first job there as newspaper cartoonist with the *News-Leader* at the age of 17. Moving to the *Arkansas Democrat* in 1941, he took a leave of absence after two years to join the Army, turning out cartoons for *Yank* and *Army Times*.

'So we're not neat'

© Arkansas Democrat

After the war, Kennedy returned to the *Arkansas Democrat* and remained with that paper. His editor preferred cartoon and editorials to be on the same subject, but this was not a fixed policy. "Occasionally, we disagree, but our policy is that I don't project any opinions that the paper disavows," he says.

These drawings by Jon Kennedy were done with an Artsign, Series 9 Finepoint No. 3 brush, using a No. 1 soft pencil for shading; and the editorial cartoonist is "still hooked on ol' timey Coquille 158-2 paper."

The specter of a former governor, replete with all his "qualifications," haunts the Arkansas landscape in this cartoon by Kennedy.

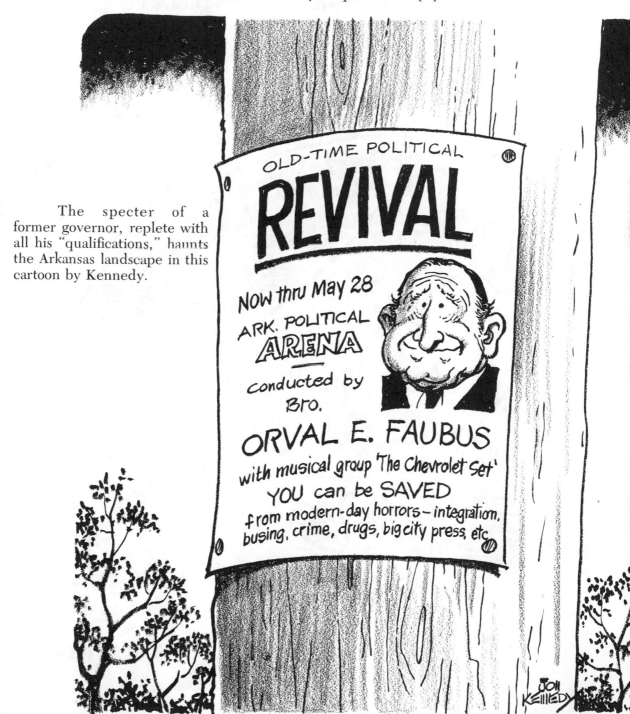

William G. ("Willy") King, born and reared in Rome, Georgia, has been with the Chattanooga (Tennessee) *Times* for more than 30 years. In addition to his editorial cartooning assignments for the *Times* he writes a weekly fishing column entitled *Wetting a Line With Willy*.

Forced by the Depression to become a school dropout, Willy spent eight years in the clothing manufacturing business before finally getting a

For Earth's Sake, Don't Leave Me!

job on a newspaper. He makes no secret of his fondness for using the symbol of Uncle Sam in much of his work.

The cartoons of Willy King, carefully done in pen and ink, clearly indicate that his is a labor of love, and that he'd do anything in the world to help his Uncle.

Who Needs Fireworks?

Jack Lanigan studied at the Art Institute of Chicago, his native city, and while exhibiting at Cape Cod, Massachusetts, during the summer of 1962, was invited to work for the *Standard Times*.

A veteran of 44 months with the Pacific Amphibious Forces during the war, and later with a bomb-testing unit at the Eniwetok atoll in the Pacific proving grounds, Lanigan, as we can see below, became concerned with such things as a Massachusetts governor and the state budget, as well as national matters.

The famous Senate Watergate Committee in a moment of repose, or during a station break, as envisioned by the editorial cartoonist and possibly some other clairvoyant TV viewers.

Jack Lanigan submits two roughs a day to his editors. Occasionally he stays up late nights thinking of an idea. His finished art is done at the office, on rough Craftint illustration boards, using Windsor Newton brushes, Pelican ink and Martin's whitener, usually taking him about five hours per drawing from start to finish.

Chick Larsen, of Newport News, Virginia, started out as a steam engineer machinist in the Navy, helping build destroyers and cruisers, and continued at that trade for ten years in civilian life.

In 1951, after attaining a bachelor of arts degree, the *Times-Dispatch* added Larsen, who is active in church affairs, to its art department and 16 years later he became its editorial cartoonist, in which capacity he has won a fair quota of awards.

'I Can't Find My Glasses'

OCT. 16 1973

Chick Larsen

Chick Larsen does from one to forty sketches a day, later finding these "thumbnails" helpful in attaining "action and composition." His finished drawings are done on Coquille board with pen and ink and No. 2 pencil, and average about an hour and a quarter to complete.

Laying bare a glaring deficiency, Larsen exposed the result of creeping inflation in this amusing drawing.

'Something's Wrong, I Can Feel It'

JAN 25 1974

© 1974

Rob Lawlor was born in Philadelphia, Pennsylvania and educated in that city. In 1972 he became editorial cartoonist for the Philadelphia *Daily News*. A former minor league baseball player in the Philadelphia A's, Dodgers, and Cards organizations, Lawlor, an admirer of L.D. Warren, applied to over a hundred newspapers for the kind of work he is now doing, even while engaged in the "national pastime."

"I make around 30 roughs a week as I view the news; editors occasionally make suggestions, but mostly the ideas are mine," he says.

The editorial cartoonist excoriates crowded conditions in a Pennsylvania prison

Here he discovered the government's star witness

"Jailbreak Heck, I Just Fell Out!"

"Senator Ervin, let me make this perfectly clear...!"

The coddling of ruthless murderers in the Middle East was more than twitted in this forceful drawing.

"And I promise I'll never do it again!"

Guernsey Le Pelley, a Harvard graduate, served in Alaska with the Air Transport Command during World War II. He studied at the Chicago Art Institute and the Evanston Academy of Fine Art, then did work for such media as the Highland Park *Press,* Lake Forest *News,* and Dallas *News,* before settling down at the *Christian Science Monitor* in 1961 as editorial cartoonist. A licensed pilot and active flyer, Le Pelley's interest also lies in the theater. He has written several off-Broadway plays and is cofounder of the summer theater at Sharon, Connecticut.

Le Pelley works with a rather tough deadline. He says, "This is partly due to the fact that the *Christian Science Monitor,* having a worldwide circulation, uses instantaneous facsimile printing at various remote offset printing plants and usually my cartoon has to be ready for the camera division in less than an hour."

Mugged?

"They said a milk bath would make me beautiful"

The Christian Science Monitor

An illegal campaign contribution by the milk industry, "in exchange for favors" was the latest scandal, and the editorial cartoonist visualized President Nixon in a rather fetching pose, before his bathroom mirror.

Trophy

Le Pelley let the U.S.A. take a breather while he went on safari to ponder a crippling strike overseas.

A prodigal son was invited to "come home, all is forgiven," during the oil shortage. (Notice that "Coal" still looked ready, willing and fairly able to fill the breech.)

© 1973 The Christian Science Monitor

"There's no fuel like an old fuel"

"The *Monitor* gives me a fairly free hand, although I am required to submit rough drawings to the editor for his approval," says Le Pelley, "*Monitor* cartooning is also somewhat specialized. I do not deal in picture ideas such as a knife in the back, or a head on the block. And I am a satirist rather than a propagandist."

Al Liederman, who was born in Rochester, New York, and makes Merrick, Long Island, his home, stepped out of high school right into a job as sports cartoonist with the Rochester *Journal American*, later working his way through night school at the Rochester Institute of Technology and the Art Students League in New York City.

"THERE'S GOOD NEWS AND THERE'S BAD NEWS"

An admirer of nearly every cartoonist when he was a child, Al was nevertheless tempted to "chuck it all" as he matured, in spite of his early success, in favor of a career as a prizefighter. Fortunately for thousands of newspaper readers in the New York metropolitan area, his mother discouraged that idea, fast.

In one crisis, anyway, all else having failed, Liederman simply asked "hard-bitten" New Yorkers to renew their faith in Santa Claus!

" WAKE UP! "

Would stiffer and stiffer assessments continue to drive business out of Gotham? Here was the way Liederman saw it.

A graphic argument for gun control, by the editorial cartoonist, showing inventiveness and originality in the handling of that well-known skyline.

THE EVICTORS

Occasionally, some members of the American Society of Editorial Cartoonists run into a problem with a "new face." This time it was Al Liederman who provided a few helpful hints in their monthly journal, as President Richard Nixon resigned and a certain Congressman from Michigan suddenly found himself thrust into the White House.

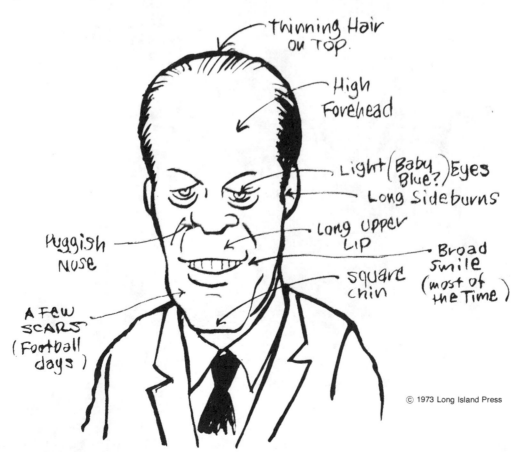

Dick Locher was born in Dubuque, Iowa, studied at the Chicago Academy of Fine Arts, then went into service during the Korean conflict, testing jet planes. Afterwards, he helped draw the *Buck Rogers* comic strip, then assisted Chester Gould with *Dick Tracy* before settling down to a job with the Chicago *Tribune*.

New comedy act

Extremely proud of his profession, Locher attributes his success to the *esprit de corps* that exists in the *Tribune* offices, where he was told, when the paper hired him, to consider himself "a member of the editorial board, completely on his own," and not to require help from anybody. "Yes, I've had a few drawings turned down after I did them, but I guess nobody can win 'em all," he says.

"... One moment, sir! Have you paid your tax on that barrel?"

This conception of a shootout at dawn, possibly in Lincoln Parks, gave many Chicagoans a hearty laugh, especially when they noticed the unlikely-looking marksman on the right was their mayor.

A Lincoln-Nixon drawing made effective by the contrast in that stark-white, spiritual quality of the statue and the dark, brooding tones of the President.

"... perhaps if you could convince more of the people just some of the time ...!"

Dick Locher gets up at 6 A.M. daily, is at the drawing board by 7 A.M., and finishes his cartoon right up to the inking before driving to the office. He uses Strathmore 3-ply smooth sheets for a finished drawing, doing them 12 inches high by 10 inches wide. No. 4 Artsign brushes, fine-line crow-quill pens, and imported heavy, thick, one coat black india ink rounds out his equipment.

"Air bags in cars ... Big deal!
We've had your mother in the back seat for years!"

"Who will ever remember Anyone gi
His life for peace?"

Ranan Lurie, a sixth-generation Israeli, who now makes his home in the United States, studied art in Jerusalem and Paris, and is a faculty member of the fine arts department at the University of Haifa, which he visits annually to lecture on political cartooning.

A regular contributor to *Newsweek,* Lurie's work is distributed internationally by *The New York Times* Special Features Syndicate, appearing in more than 140 newspapers, and has won for him awards from the Montreal Salon, the Newspaper Guild of New York, and the National Cartoonists Society.

Many celebrities have sat for oil paintings or caricatures by Ranan Lurie, including Nelson Rockefeller, Melvin Laird, William P. Rogers, and two Senators from his home state (Connecticut), Abraham Ribicoff and Lowell Weicker.

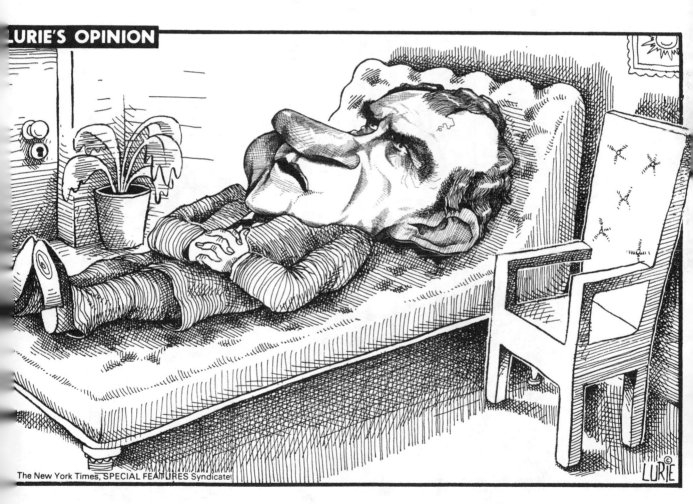

LURIE'S OPINION

The New York Times, SPECIAL FEATURES Syndicate

"DOCTOR... NO ONE WANTS TO LISTEN TO ME ANYMORE."

THE LONDON SUNDAY TIMES

Typical Lurie portrait-caricatures on this magazine cover drawing include (from left to right) Henry Kissinger, Golda Meir, Anwar Sadat, Kissinger again, and on the table an unidentified sum of money.

"The only difference between a good editorial writer and a good political cartoonist is that the editorial writer doesn't know how to draw," says Ranan Lurie. Before starting work on a cartoon, Lurie searches for the message he wishes to convey by reading accumulated facts and steeping himself in much background material.

"Every contract with a syndicate I have had includes a clear-cut definition of the absolute independence I should have from every point of view—analytically, graphically, and humorously," Lurie continues. "The fact is that all the very best cartoonists in this country are politically independent, and get staunch support from newspapers who give them that carte blanche."

This Lurie cow, drawn during the milk scandal in the Nixon administration, amused readers with its anatomical license. Notice the kind of grass it was feeding on.

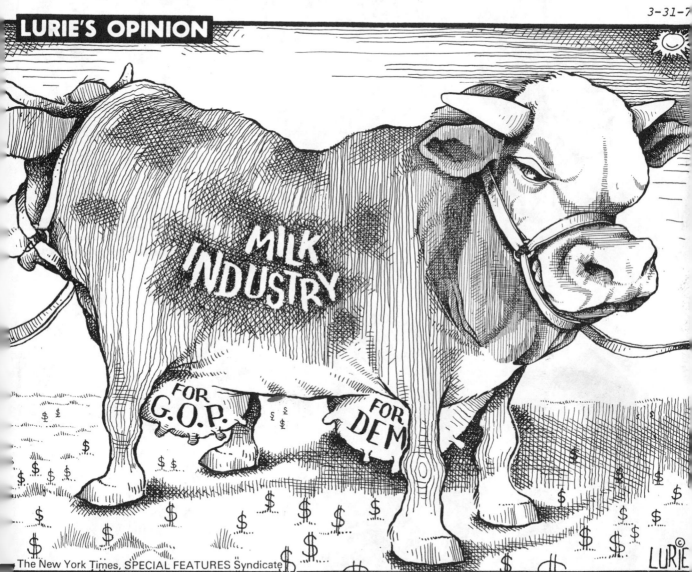

AN EQUAL OPPORTUNITY EMPLOYER

LOS ANGELES TIMES

A gallery of portrait-caricatures by Ranan Lurie.

VICE PRESIDENT GERALD FORD
DER SPIEGEL

RON ZEIGLER,

INDIRA GANDHI. PRIME MINISTER OF INDIA

PRESIDENT HAFEZ-AL-ASSAD OF SYRIA
THE PHILADELPHIA BULLETIN

SENATOR CHARLES H. PERCY

ALEXANDER SOLZHENITSYN

Has Lurie ever met the "impossible" subject? His answer:

"No, there is no one I can't caricature. However, the older a person is, the easier it is to establish his features and personality."

It's questionable whether this picture made anybody in the Kremlin laugh, but certainly Russian cartoon-buffs must have at least appreciated the likeness of Communist Party chief Leonid Brezhnev.

Caricaturists sometimes run a risk of getting socked on the jaw. Has anyone ever mentioned doing such a thing to him? "No, I was never threatened. I did see some sour faces, but generally speaking, since my subjects are mainly politicians, their general attitude is, 'If you can't lick him, join him,' and they become ever nicer guys."

In this cartoon Ranan Lurie shows a U.S. Vice President as quite a swinger. (Maybe every golfer should have a club like that!)

12-15-73

LURIE'S OPINION

FROM "NIXON RATED CARTOONS" B

Does Lurie draw a person the same way a second or third tim[e]
"The same person may appear sympathetic in one caricature and nasty [in]
the next. It depends on the message of the cartoon which sometimes may
condemn a person and at another time praise him."

LURIE'S OPINION
THE WHEELER-DEALER

THE LONDON SUNDAY TIMES

HENRY KISSINGER

THE LONDON SUNDAY TIMES

© 1974 The New York Times, SPECIAL FEATURES Syndicate   4-14-74

RANAN LURIE

WEST EAST

As Thomas Griffin, former editor of *Life* magazine, says, "Lurie is almost never vindictive or moralistic; what saves him from blandness is the sharpness of his judgment, conveyed by metaphor."

"COME, COME, IT'S ONLY ONE SMALL JUMP!"

Reg Manning arrived in Arizona as a child and became staff artist for the *Arizona Republic* shortly after graduating from high school. He never really wanted to draw political cartoons, but in the mid-1930's he couldn't resist taking "pen jabs" at Adolf Hitler.

A Pulitzer Prize winner in 1951, as well as recipient of many other awards, Manning's studio in Scottsdale, Arizona, is entirely surrounded by desert landscaping and affords him a grand view of famed Camelback Mountain.

Another Species Endangered By Crumbling Shells

WINNER, FREEDOMS FOUNDATION ABRAHAM LINCOLN AWARD, 1972
ARIZONA REPUBLIC, JULY 12, 1971

If the view from Reg Manning's studio offers him an opportunity for escape, it doesn't show in his work.

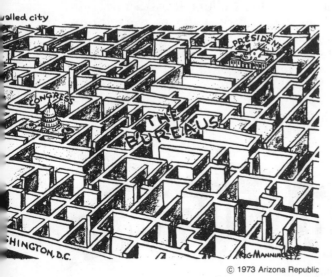

A "honeycomb" of a drawing, maybe enough to give a bureaucrat claustrophobia.

Dam!

Here the editorial cartoonist called his readers' attention to a local problem quite vital (and expensive) to them.

An observation on livestock, of the *Homo sapiens* variety.

Doug Marlette was born in Greensboro, North Carolina, and educated in that state as well as in Florida. While attending Florida State University, he drew cartoons which were distributed by the College Press Service and used in student newspapers throughout the country. Later he worked professionally for the Orlando *Sentinel Star* and the St. Petersburg *Times* before joining the staff of the Charlotte, (North Carolina) *Observer* in 1972.

Why is there such a scarcity of conservatives among artists on the editorial pages? Marlette believes that it is because cartoonists are, by their very nature, rabble rousers. "Our drawings are at their very best when we are attacking the status quo," he says.

Like Tony Auth, Marlette cites the Vietnam war as the event that "liberated cartoonists to draw politicians the way they really are, as demagogues. All the things we were taught back in Laurel, Mississippi, about the sanctity of the Constitution turned out to be a lie, the politicians just didn't believe it," he says. Marlette continues, "We've had a tendency to idolize politicians, to put Presidents on pedestals. All that was undermined by the war, and then Watergate. The 'straight' papers are coming to terms with reality, and now the thoughts that were always unthinkable are being drawn."

A vulture, instead of a cuckoo bird, tells the story of a bloody South American coup d'état.

A strange bird amidst all those high-flying storks illustrated a news report that seemed depressing to the editorial cartoonist.

NEWS ITEM:

N.C. INFANT MORTALITY RATE THIRD HIGHEST IN NATION

Good likenesses of five-ninths of the Supreme Court, plus good lettering, combined in helping lampoon the controversy over obscenity.

Another controversial issue, that of capital punishment in his own state, was handled poignantly by Marlette.

Doug Marlette draws directly with various shades of pencils, then inks in with a radiograph technical pen having a variety of points, or using a Windsor Newton No. 2 brush. Having an editor who "has a very good ability to visualize," he merely describes an idea before drawing it up. "My editor has veto power over an idea, but that is usually exercised when he thinks one doesn't work effectively, seldom over content, since we are in general philosophic agreement on most issues," he says.

Bill Mauldin was born in New Mexico and grew up on a ranch near Phoenix, Arizona. His first job as an artist was at the age of 12, drawing posters for a rodeo. While in high school at Phoenix, he took a correspondence course in cartooning and sold his first cartoon for $10. After high school, he went to Chicago where he worked as a truck driver, dishwasher, and menu designer to pay for his studies at the Art Institute.

Mauldin served with the U.S. Army during World War II in the 45th Infantry Division. He saw enough action in Italy, France, and Germany to earn a Purple Heart Decoration. The war served as a background for his famous "Up Front" Willie and Joe cartoons that appeared regularly in *Stars and Stripes*.

The winner of Pulitzer prizes in 1944 and 1958, his books include *Mud, Mules and Mountains*, *This Damn Tree Leaks*, *Back Home*, *A Sort of a Saga*, and *I've Decided I Want My Seat Back*. From 1958 to 1962 Mauldin was editorial cartoonist for the St. Louis *Post Dispatch*. Since then he has been with the Chicago *Sun-Times*.

Mauldin's most recent award was the Charles Huart prize for newspaper cartoons, from the French Foundation for Art and Research.

"WELL, HOWDY THERE, NEIGHBOR!"

"...THE STRIPED ONE IS FOR RIDING DURING THE BUS RIC THIS GREEN ONE IS FOR CROSSING THE TEACHERS' PICKE

This world famous "Up Front" cartoon by Bill Mauldin, won him the 1944 Pulitzer Prize.

"*resh, spirited American troops, flushed with victory, are bring-* *in thousands of hungry, ragged, battle-weary prisoners . . .*"

(News item)

At Yale University where Mauldin gave a course in political cartooning, he demonstrated ideas for characterizing political personalities with just a few strokes of his pencil. Here to the right are Mauldin's instant Lyndon B. Johnson, Charles de Gaulle, Richard Nixon, Franklin D. Roosevelt, Fidel Castro, and Adolph Hitler.

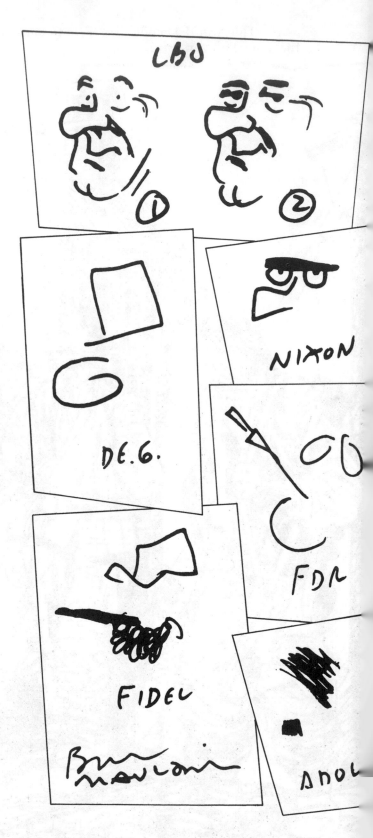

Frank Miller, a native of Kansas, won his Pulitzer Prize in 1963. He is often asked how he can be "flip and funny" about such things as H-Bombs, fall-out shelters, and World War III. His stock answer is a quote of Abe Lincoln's, when the Great Emancipator was asked a similar question following a horrendous setback for Union forces during the Civil War. "Can't you see? If I didn't laugh, I would cry."

THE MACHINERY FOR PEACE IS COMPLEX

A graduate of the University of Kansas and the Kansas City Art Institute, Miller served with the Third Army in Europe during World War II, and with the Seventh Infantry Division (artillery) in Korea.

The style of Frank Miller is free and loose and thoroughly individual, obviously the result of long years of experience.

IT IS WONDERFUL HOW WE GET SIMPLE ANSWERS TO COMPLICATED QUESTIONS

THE POLITICIAN'S IMAGE HASN'T IMPROVED MUCH LATELY

Here, the editorial cartoonist wasn't aiming at any one Boss Tweed in particular, but at the entire breed everywhere.

Mark Nadrowski was born in Buffalo, New York, and graduated from Notre Dame. He started contributing editorial cartoons to the Rochester *Democrat-Chronicle* when he was 16.

An amateur pianist, Mark happened to be visiting the library in his native city in 1961 when he chanced across an exhibition of original drawings by Bruce Shanks, editorial cartoonist of the Buffalo *Evening News*, which inspired him. Later, meeting Shanks, he received much good advice on techniques. Nadrowski is a voracious reader, perusing "everything from the census to the annual federal budget."

'*Morning, Figby. Did Detroit recall your car, too?*'
© Democrat and Chronicle

Mark Nadrowski does his drawings 12 X 14 inches, using Grumbacher sable brushes, and ordinary lithograph crayons. When it comes to caricature, he studies as many photos of a subject as possible.

'Does our tin lizzy really belong in the space age?'
© Democrat and Chronicle

Obsolescence in the fight against sickness is satirized here by the editorial cartoonist.

A dig at the Postmaster General, illustrated this time without any wheels at all!

Zoom, roar, zoom!
© Democrat and Chronicle

Leonard Matheson Norris, of the Vancouver (British Columbia) *Sun,* was a captain in the Royal Canadian Electrical and Mechanical Engineers, as well as an editor, writer, illustrator, and art director. Born in England, he has received the National Newspaper Award, as well as many other prizes. In 1973, he was granted an honorary Doctorate of Laws degree from the University of Windsor, Ontario.

...on modern painters

't's only vin du pays *. . . we're a bit strapped as Cecil is between Canada Council grants.'*

Norris on this and succeeding pages focuses on some typical subjects, clearly proving that comic art has a place on the editorial pages, so long as it's witty, well-drawn, and *meaningful.*

...on culture

'. . . as Rodney so aptly put it, mere words simply cannot do justice in describing the magnificent Festival ballet . . .'

A good-natured spoofing of dilettantes by the editorial cartoonist.
The more complex our civilization grows, the more complex our reasons for its faults, says Norris in effect.

Norris on the environment

'. . . a hale and healthy worm, Mrs. Phelps, is living proof of the complete absence of dangerous sprays . . .'

...on youth

I know you wouldn't think it to look at him . . . but he has a good job in the Montreal head office of an active, go-ahead, government-sponsored, young Canadian company.

Worry about yourselves, instead, oldsters were advised in this cartoon.

Do we *really* have to worry about these the little wiseguys, Len Norris asks us here?

Badgered by various newspaper editors to come to work for them, this very talented pen-and-ink artist resisted all offers until one came at just the right moment. "The rat race was becoming unbearable. I wanted to play golf and smell the flowers," says Leonard Matheson Norris.

...on children

What long words it is in one of them for a cat to spell demanded!

John Pierotti started his career in 1927 with the New York *Telegram*. Later he went to the Washington *Post*, *P.M.*, the New York *Star*, and finally the New York *Post*. He is a former president of the National Cartoonists Society and has won seven Page One awards, as well as numerous other honors for his work.

Says Pierotti, "I always get very excited when I get a good idea and can't wait to finish it. Usually, this takes about an hour. I draw very simply on purpose, and try to use ideas that tell the whole story, without any labels if possible." Occasionally, he has been at odds with editors over some of his ideas, and he believes that "some beauties weren't published." One thing is for certain, though: John Pierotti's grandchildren love *everything* he draws!

An excellent study of an almost mortally wounded elephant, by the editorial cartoonist.

"ET TU, NIXON?"

This probably was one of the most powerful drawings on the war in Indochina. Pierotti simply takes a news item and gives it a literal, graphic translation.

John Pierotti starts out by sketching in his drawing with pencil on a sheet of coquille or gloras paper. Then, after "cleaning up," he inks in with brushes and applies William Korn lithograph crayon for shading.

Eldon Pletcher was brought up on a farm at Goshen, Indiana, but claims he still can't draw horses, cows and chickens "on account of having the opposite of a photographic eye." He attended the Chicago Academy of Fine Arts in 1941-1942, went overseas during the war as a demolition expert and returned to this country afterwards to start drawing for the Sioux City (Iowa) *Journal* in 1949, remaining there for 17 years and becoming known as "Pletch the Wretch" after a reader dubbed him thus.

ONE OF THESE DAYS. . . !

In 1966 Pletch became editorial cartoonist for the New Orleans *Times-Picayune.* "In my more than two decades in this profession, I have never had a drawing 'killed,' except on account of fast-moving events," he says, "possibly because I have a conservative philosophy and have always worked for conservative papers."

Next He'll Be Wanting To Recall The Government

Unanswered questions

Tragedy in the news impelled the editorial cartoonist to point up the need for adequate fire protection in *all* kinds of public housing.

Rault Center Holocaust (4 die–several more later which pointed up to the Nation the hazards of high rise building.

Eldon Pletcher uses Bainbridge coquille boards (rough surface), #3 or #4 red sable brushes, and lithograph crayons—both sticks and pencils—for his middle tones. He has also become addicted to Grafix paper on which the middle tones (screened half-tone effects) appear when a chemical is applied.

Art Poinier originally a sports cartoonist with the Columbus *Dispatch*, also worked for the Cleveland *Press* and the Des Moines (Iowa) *Register* and *Tribune*. Born in Oak Park, Illinois, Poinier became editorial cartoonist for the Detroit *Free Press* in 1939, continuing to draw the nationally syndicated comic strip, *Jitter*, which he had started three years before.

Poinier was commissioned a Naval Air Combat Intelligence officer during World War II, and served several tours of combat duty. After finishing service, he returned to his old job and in 1951 joined the Detroit *News*.

© Detroit News

From the vantage point atop the Washington Monument, we perceive the then ex-governor of New York State looking for a place to land, just prior to his being named Vice President.

U.F.O. SIGHTING OVER THE WHITE HOUSE.

For fresh air, every Friday evening Art Poinier rushes out to his apple orchard six miles from Ann Arbor, Michigan, where he enjoys being a weekend farmer.

Alan Pratt came out of Portland, Oregon, virtually following in his father's footsteps to become a newspaper artist. He "lugged a rifle around the Rhineland" during World War II, then spent a year in Japan, "teaching police how to police," before returning to the Northwest and getting a job with the Seattle *Times;* however, said job only consisted of retouching photos, making maps, and doing other assorted jobs.

'CHANGE OF TIDE'

In 1957, the mantle of editorial cartoonist was finally thrust upon Pratt and he was quick to accept it. A compulsive fisherman and ecologist, his avocation is being "litter and pollution editor" of the *Wretched Mess News*, a tiny periodical out of West Yellowstone, Montana.

Two editorial cartoons by Pratt on the subjects of energy and ecology. Alan Pratt's work is unaffected, unpretentious, and cartooning in the great, comic style, except that it leaves a reader *thinking*.

Sam Rawls, editorial cartoonist for the Palm Beach (Florida) *Post*, was born in Clarksdale, Mississippi, and graduated from Fort Lauderdale High School in Florida and from Florida State College. An outdoors enthusiast and conservation booster, he is active among youth groups, coaching football and baseball.

In 1972 and 1973, Rawls was named Cartoonist of the Year by the University of Florida. The state has accorded him many other awards for his outstanding art work. "Papers weren't combing the countryside in search of editorial cartoonists, as I discovered early," says Rawls, and he was about to pass on to some other field of endeavor. But his wife urged him to try it anyway because "she knew that's what I wanted."

'Shhh — FBI!'

A spoof of the United States Postal Service by the editorial cartoonist.

An emaciated Uncle Sam, designed by Rawls for the lean years, hunts vainly for goodies in this version of the Horn of Plenty.

Sam Rawls draws on Grafix craft tint paper, using #1 and #2 sable brushes and a crow-quill pen for occasional cross-hatching. It takes him from two to five hours to complete a drawing.

Dennis Renault, who joined McClatchy Newspapers in 1971, also does free-lance political cartoons and comic art for such national publications as the *Saturday Review, Playboy,* and *Ladies Home Journal.* He studied graphic arts and political science at the University of Southern California, in Los Angeles, taking time out for a two-year hitch in the armed forces.

"The most satisfying cartoons I've done are those representing exploited members of society such as farm laborers and their working children—in other words, the weak and powerless," says Renault.

Black Samson

A one, two, three editorial cartoon: you look, you read, you get hot and bothered!

'I . . . . Am Sorry . . . . Doctor Frankenstein . . . . I Will Return . . . . To My Coffin . . . .'

An interpretation of the overthrow in Chile in 1973 that might have given some of his readers the *chills*.

FREEDOM AND DEMOCRACY

SOUTH AMERICAN DICTATORS

© Dennis Renault

'They Get Ideas From The United States; We Get Arms.'

Dennis Renault's drawings are done on 11 X 14 inch two-ply paper, usually coquille, with a #3 sable brush, and different "tools" when volume is required—crayons, or screen for shading. He bike-rides 10 miles to work every morning and is completely on his own as far as ideas are concerned.

John Riedell, born on a farm in Lake View, Iowa, once milked cows, herded cattle, and spaded thistles to buy drawing paper. Graduating from high school, he joined the Navy in 1949, serving aboard the destroyer-tender U.S.S. *Piedmont,* and drawing a comic feature for the Honolulu *Advertiser* while stationed at fleet headquarters in Pearl Harbor.

A former radio announcer, who taught journalism and cartooning from 1958 to 1967 in the United States and British Honduras (now Belize), Riedell has received seven Freedom Foundation awards for his work.

Here Riedell demonstrates how he appeals to readers through various emotions:

It Shrunk

Amusement, as the dollar shrinks, and with it our first President's shirt.

U.S.S. PUEBLO

Despair, as his country comes out second best in a naval confrontation off North Korea.

John Riedell claims to have tried using just about every type of illustration board and paper manufactured, in his long, distinguished career.

Hy Rosen, frequently found standing on his head, is simply practicing yoga, not trying to get ideas for his editorial cartoons. A graduate of the State University of New York, and a three-year veteran of World War II, he studied at the Chicago Art Institute and the Art Students League in New York.

As *Hy Rosen* Sees It

" CHECK YOUR OIL...? "

Rosen started with the Albany (New York) *Times-Union* in 1945 and has won a number of awards for his work, including a Professional Journalism Fellowship from Stamford University in 1966. He enjoys keeping an eye on the seat of government in his own home state of New York, perhaps because he worked right there in the capital.

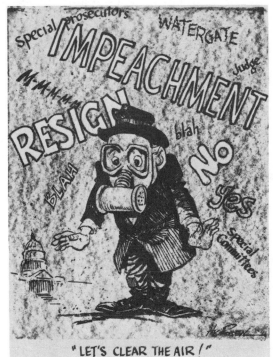

"LET'S CLEAR THE AIR!"

Smog, or a heavy layer of deception during Richard Nixon's final days in Washington—the editorial cartoonist apparently couldn't decide which.

"HAPPY FIRST QUARTER TO YOU, BIG DADDY!"

Good news for fuel company stockholders, and some of Rosen's readers who didn't even own a share, probably liked this cartoon, too!

Hy Rosen shows one to three rough sketches of his ideas per day, and there has never been any argument about them. He draws on Grafix or Glarco paper, using #3 brushes, #B6 pens and lithograph crayon. It takes him about three hours to finish a cartoon.

Arnold Roth, whose work appears with regular frequency in such publications as *Punch, Sports Illustrated, TV Guide,* the *National Lampoon,* and *Playboy,* was born in Philadelphia and studied at the School of Industrial Arts in the city of brotherly love.

Beginning his professional career in 1951, Roth has successfully authored such tomes as *Arnold Roth's Crazy Book of Science* and *Pick a Peck of Puzzles.* A chronic sufferer from backaches, he frequently works standing up "to keep from being mistaken from Toulouse-Lautrec." He has received awards from the Philadelphia Artists Guild, and Art Directors Clubs in New York and Chicago, among others.

If you get the impression that the 37th President of the United States is a bit short in stature in this spread, you are correct, but it is Mr. Nixon nevertheless. Arnold Roth, its creator, belongs to the modern schools of cartooning which, like Stanislavsky in the theater, believes that the person portrayed must emerge from the *real* person. Thus, Roth's Chief Executive, though shrunken in height, appears to be somewhat more wistful and lovable than in real life. Roth follows no particular process for thinking up cartoon ideas, merely hopes that readers will find his finished work entertaining. He draws with all kinds of pens—"coquille to post office types"—and uses brushes (Windsor and Newton sables) for water col-

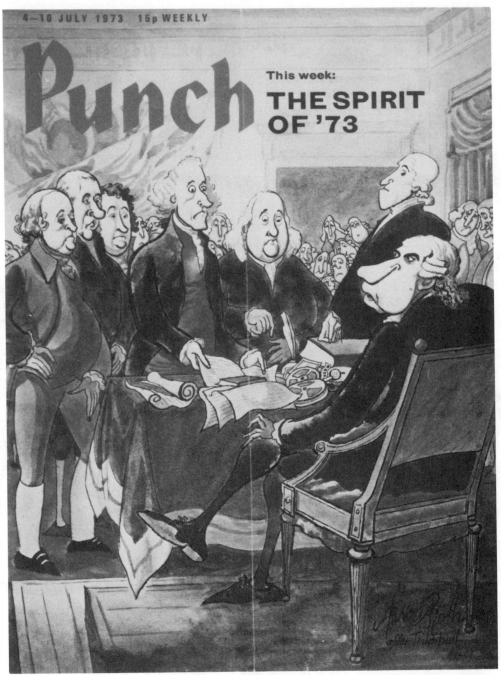

4—10 JULY 1973   15p WEEKLY

Punch

This week:
THE SPIRIT OF '73

oring only. His paper, sometimes scratchboard, is of the finest quality because many of his originals are quickly bought up by collectors, and therefore Roth believes it only fair that they endure. He enjoys drawing for *Punch* on account of the high quality of satire it has attained under a new editor who frequently calls on him for "subject issues."

Vic Runtz, of Arnprior, Ontario, crossed over the border to become the first editorial cartoonist for the Bangor (Maine) *Daily News,* a position he has held since the late 1950's. Just prior to the attack on Pearl Harbor, Runtz enlisted in the Canadian Navy and four years later began studying drawing at Sir George Williams College and the Montreal Artists School, both in Montreal. Working in an office, rather than at the paper, he says, "I try to make my point with humor and a light touch. It can be just as effective as a bludgeon."

ASK THEM *IF JUSTICE IS SERVED*

"Honest . . . it's not 'streaking' . . . it's the cost of living . . . can't even find a barrel to wear . . ."

Nude figures are permissible in a family newspaper, provided they are drawn "funny," as Runtz has done here. Anyway, it turns out this wasn't just a college kid cutting up, and an officer of the law had the culprit in tow.

Everybody loves a baby and this cartoon of one with its main staple practically out of reach undoubtedly made a lot of people in Maine angry with the Milk Lobby and the Nixon administration.

If Baby's going to grow up to be President . . .

"Look, Ma . . . no hands!"

Everybody loves to see a happy, free-wheeling boy, too, but not as he's about to come a cropper (as this one is), for reasons beyond his control.

Vic Runtz submits several roughs to his editor each day, then does his finished drawings on Grafix, or other good grade Bristol board, plate finish, using Windsor & Newton series 7 brushes (sizes 2,3,4) and Gilliot's 170 pen nibs.

Bob Saylor, of the Houston *Post,* demonstrates the versatility of the modern editorial/political cartoonist in these two samples of his work.

Of this first one, a tribute to the 36th President of the United States, Saylor says that Lyndon B. Johnson's "attachments to his Texas roots, the fact that he considered himself a Texan rather than an urban personality,

led him to create this drawing to symbolize the geographical background. This is the way I think LBJ would like to be remembered."

Saylor adds that he discarded his first idea of drawing an empty Western saddle because he felt that it did not sufficiently mark the measure of the man. "The riderless horse, however, carries the symbolism further without complicating its message," he says. The drawing attracted considerable response in the *Post's* letters-to-the-editor column, according to Al Shires, Assistant Managing Editor.

Here is Bob Saylor, in a completely different style!

"This Jan. 27, 1974 drawing points up the absence of citizen interest in the current constitutional convention in Austin, Texas," says

'Wake up . . . It's your vehicle'

Saylor's editor. "Although Texans generally have agreed the past few years that the state constitution needs updating, few have participated in the current meetings."

David Earle Seavey had to get baseball out of his system before deciding on a career in art. Good enough to receive encouragement from big-league scouts, Dave traveled to Florida one winter to try out with the Washington Senators, although at the age of 14 he had already been working as sports cartoonist for the *Daily Democrat* in Dover, New Hampshire.

BUREAUCRATIC SPENDING EXCESSES

In this cartoon, Dave Seavey set forth the notion that an exiled Russian author's pen could prove mightier than the hammer and sickle.

ALEXANDRE SOLZHENITSYN—AUTHOR

Failing to get that baseball contract, Seavey concentrated on winning a national high school art competition, began studying at the School of Visual Arts in New York City, and worked briefly as an illustrator for a greeting cards company before connecting with the *National Observer*.

Many Seavey readers must have felt that they were being sucked into those horrendous gears themselves.

TAXPAYERS COMMENT

The skeletal figure hovering over the scene suggests that Seavey himself may not be too crazy about auto racing.

INDIANAPOLIS 500

Bruce Shanks, born and brought up in Buffalo, New York, is naturally the pride of that city's *Evening News*, with 11 Freedom Foundation awards, 11 Page One awards, a Christopher Medal, and last but not least the prestigious Pulitzer.

During World War II, Shanks served in the Air Force Intelligence alongside another cartoonist, Herbert L. Block (Herblock). Now retired and living in Boca Raton, Florida, he estimates that he did almost 25,000 editorial cartoons in his lifetime!

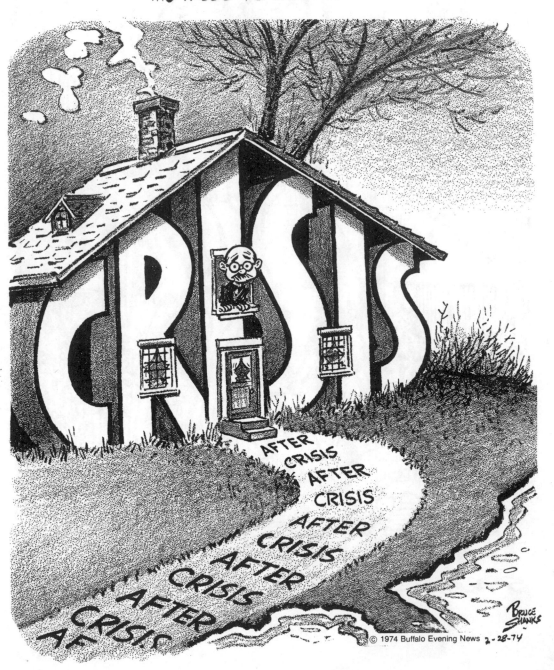

THE HOUSE WE LIVE IN

LAND OF THE FREE?

Two puzzlers by the editorial cartoonist: when would something be done about the first—?

© 1973 Buffalo Evening News 2-1-73

LONGEST GAME ON RECORD

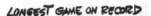

—and how to keep either side from making a move in the second!

© 1972 Buffalo Evening News 7-31-72

The great hulking figure with the sword reminded readers that those other little fellers needed all the support they could get.

Bruce Shanks proves in this unforgettable portrait of the 16th President of the United States that an editorial cartoonist, to be at the top of his profession, must be resourceful, innovative, and full of surprises for his readers.

'—And That Government of the People—'

FOURSCORE AND SEVEN YEARS AGO OUR FATHERS BROUGHT FORTH ON THIS CONTINENT A NEW NATION CONCEIVED IN LIBERTY AND DEDICATED TO THE PROPOSITION THAT ALL MEN ARE CREATED EQUAL. NOW WE ARE ENGAGED IN A GREAT CIVIL WAR TESTING WHETHER THAT NATION OR ANY NATION SO CONCEIVED AND SO DEDICATED, CAN LONG ENDURE. WE ARE MET ON A GREAT BATTLEFIELD OF THAT WAR. WE HAVE COME TO DEDICATE A PORTION OF THAT FIELD AS A FINAL RESTING PLACE FOR THOSE WHO HERE GAVE THEIR LIVES THAT THAT NATION MIGHT LIVE. IT IS ALTOGETHER FITTING AND PROPER THAT WE SHOULD DO THIS. BUT IN A LARGER SENSE WE CANNOT DEDICATE, WE CANNOT CONSECRATE, WE CANNOT HALLOW THIS GROUND. THE BRAVE MEN, LIVING AND DEAD WHO STRUGGLED HERE HAVE CONSECRATED IT FAR ABOVE OUR POOR POWER TO ADD OR DETRACT. THE WORLD WILL LITTLE NOTE NOR LONG REMEMBER WHAT WE SAY HERE, BUT CAN NEVER FORGET WHAT THEY DID HERE. IT IS FOR US THE LIVING RATHER TO BE DEDICATED HERE TO THE UNFINISHED WORK WHICH THEY WHO FOUGHT HERE HAVE THUS FAR SO NOBLY ADVANCED. IT IS RATHER FOR US TO BE HERE DEDICATED TO THE GREAT TASK REMAINING BEFORE US—THAT FROM THESE HONORED DEAD WE TAKE INCREASED DEVOTION TO THAT CAUSE FOR WHICH THEY GAVE THE LAST FULL MEASURE OF DEVOTION—THAT WE HERE HIGHLY RESOLVE THAT THESE DEAD SHALL NOT HAVE DIED IN VAIN, THAT THIS NATION UNDER GOD SHALL HAVE A NEW BIRTH OF FREEDOM AND THAT GOVERNMENT OF THE PEOPLE, BY THE PEOPLE, FOR THE PEOPLE, SHALL NOT PERISH FROM THE EARTH

Buffalo Evening News, February 12, 1954

Freedoms Foundation Award — 1954

Bob Sullivan took advantage of the G.I. bill, following his stint flying bombers over Germany for the Air Force during World War II, to absorb a liberal arts education at Syracuse University. Finishing the course, Sullivan failed to find the welcome mat out at any newspaper office and spent the next 15 years as an industrial engineer until at last the Worcester *Telegram* and *Gazette* beckoned. About editorial cartoonists, he says, "Unfortunately, they are a very exclusive bunch that rarely seem to retire or get removed from office for any reason including high crimes and misdemeanors." His fondest hope is that the politicians and bureaucrats he loathes will regret he hadn't stuck to industrial engineering.

© Worcester Telegram

Death of a Salesman

One-time top Presidential domestic advisor John Ehrlichman defended his role with the White House "plumbers" and the editorial cartoonist didn't seem too impressed.

'Well, in order to save it, we had to destroy it a little.'

© Worcester Telegram

Sullivan didn't seem impressed with "new guidelines for low-cost housing" set forth by the Nixon administration, either.

'There! THAT ought to do it!'

After the morning editorial conference at Bob Sullivan's paper there is a cartoon conference at which time he presents his rough sketches of ideas. Following selection, he does a finish directly on the premises, using single-tone Grafix coquille illustration boards, #2 brushes of any make, and occasionally a crow-quill pen.

Paul Szep, a native of Ontario, Canada, and 1974 Pulitzer Prize winner, had this said about him by Tom Wicker, the well-known columnist for *The New York Times:* "Years ago when I was a young editorial writer on the Nashville *Tennessean,* I used to discuss cartoon ideas every morning with Tom Little, the *Tennessean's* great editorial page cartoonist. Little was the gleeful perpetrator of such wicked drawings as one of an Eisenhower golf ball sailing over the horizon in pursuit of the first Soviet sputnik; and from Little I picked up the lasting idea that the best editorial cartoons are those that need the least caption—those in which the drawing itself is the message.

"That is not the least of what I like about Paul Szep, an ex-hockey pro, who had his teeth knocked out in the Canadian minor leagues, got the message, and became an artist. Most of the cartoons Szep draws daily for the Boston *Globe* are not mere illustrations of one-line quips, or bloodless representations of bloodless statesmen bandying sterile words; instead, Szep gives you an immediate body-check into the boards."

"Whatsoever house I enter, there will I go for the benefit of the sick, refraining from all wrongdoing or corruption."

Thus goes the Hippocratic oath, as set forth in part during the sixth century, determining a code of ethics for the practice of medicine. But, in modern times, gazing about him in his own state, Paul Szep saw members of the profession greedily exploiting, for their own personal gain, a health insurance plan that, good, bad, or indifferent, had been set up to provide hospitals with a stable source of income and to help meet rising Medicare costs.

The editorial cartoonist's own feelings in the matter may be seen in the expressions he has given those doctors robbing the till.

STAND IN LINE AND WAIT YOUR TURN LIKE GENTLEMEN

© The Boston Globe

Again, it's possible that Szep, who studied at the Ontario School of Art, was revealing his own personal sentiments about an organized group betraying a position of trust to operate for its own gain. The police he has drawn certainly appear to be anything but square-shooting Dick Tracy types.

There they were, the boys in blue, "New York's finest," having broken up a drug ring and taken into custody a fortune in heroin. "One of the greatest feats ever accomplished by any law enforcement agency in the fight against crime," proclaimed civic leaders proudly. Then, suddenly all was gone, not the police or civic leaders, just the heroin—$16,000,000 worth!

"THIS IS THE POLICE ... GIVE UP ... YOU'RE SURROUNDED!"

© The Boston Globe

Szep says, "To the *Globe's* credit, they have never imposed limitations on my creative freedom. I show my editor a rough, which he checks for libel and/or bad taste. In the course of a year, we may also show the lawyers a cartoon. Obviously, one learns to discipline himself. The *Globe* and I have a very successful marriage; we disagree very little editorially, and when that happens, they either run the cartoon on the editorial page or on the Op-Ed page."

Paul Szep draws on Grafix duo shade #224 and #232 paper, using Windsor & Newton Series 7, 4, and 5 brushes, and Gilliot-Montblanc pens. The size of his drawings is 10½·X 11½ inches.

VENUS

The Boston Globe

Bob Taylor of the Dallas *Times-Herald*, was born in Stockton, California, brought up in Los Angeles and San Francisco, and attended the University of Sacramento. An Air Force veteran, he is another example of an editorial cartoonist who started out drawing for the sports pages before turning to work that he considered "far more significant."

© Bob Taylor

Taylor has won awards from the National Conference of Christians and Jews, the Southwest Journalist Forum, and the Dallas Press Club, among others.

This concept of the Chief Executive trying to act beguiling in the halls of Congress might have dismayed Bob Taylor's readers had they detected about their representatives the $weet $mell of $ucce$$, too.

Merle Randolph Tingley may not be well known in Canada under that name, but mention "Ting," and immediately there is recognition on the part of almost everyone. A former engineer for a power plant in northern Quebec, Ting joined the army during "Hitler's War," only to be put to work drawing for a service weekly. After his discharge, he motorcycled across Canada, trying to find a newspaper that would use his services, finally landing with the London (Ontario) *Free Press*. He left to run his own syndicate and his cartoons appear in a number of daily papers and weeklies internationally.

Did a Prime Minister seeking re-election have strictly honorable intentions, Ting wondered in this cartoon. (And that girl seemed to be wondering, too!)

"TIME TO DRINK YOUR MILKYPOO AND GO TO THE LATRINE"

Naturally, war veteran Ting enjoyed spoofing the above news item.

A far-from-dumb Indian gave Canadian readers a big laugh in this Ting cartoon.

"...AN' REMEMBER, MAC, WITH INFLATION, *BEADS AN' TRINKETS* DON'T CUT AS MUCH ICE AS THEY DID MANY MOONS AGO"

© Portage La Prairie Daily Graphic 2/12/74

John Trever was educated at Syracuse University, where he majored in English literature, political science, and art. A cartoonist for the daily campus newspaper, he delayed his debut in professional journalism by enlisting in the Air Force.

Trever, who drifted into the profession by winning a national drawing contest at the age of 13, (copying Walt Kelly's *Pogo*), joined Sentinel Newspapers after leaving the service. His work appears in many periodicals, much of it on the subject of local Colorado politics, and he regards himself as one whose philosophy is "libertarian, with a strong dose of free-market economics."

"Sorry, if you fellows want windfall profits, you'll just have to go into politics...."

"All set, dear ... Tax forms, instructions, paper, pencils, erasers, calculator, cancelled checks, receipts, coffee — and inspiration!"

Trever illustrates a perfect blending of comic art and editorial cartooning in these two examples of his work, one a sly reference to President Nixon's well-known income tax problems during his administration, and the other a take-off on a popular TV panel show.

John Trever believes his philosophy suits him ideally for his profession, "since editorial cartooning is usually negative and debunking, and we shall always be afflicted with governments."

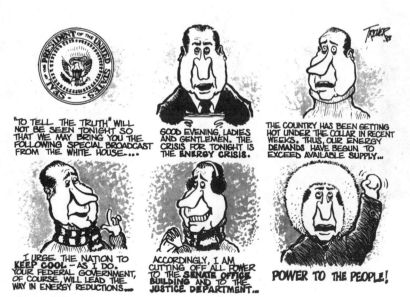

Corky Francisco Flores Trinidad, Jr., editorial cartoonist for the Honolulu *Star-Bulletin*, and the Los Angeles *Times Syndicate*, was born in Manila, Philippine Islands. His work is signed simply "Corky" and under that name he is known in hundreds of newspapers throughout the world.

Recipient of a foreign journalism award from the University of California, and the Montreal Salon of Cartoons, both in 1967, Corky is also the creator and author of the comic strip "Nguyen Charlie." He lives in Honolulu.

ULSTER

Sincerity, or depth of emotion, is the great quality found in Corky Trinidad's work, which is characterized by a simple, almost primitive style. We can immediately see it is not slickness of technique, or a trick of the drawing trade, that makes our hearts go out to this lone figure in the Cambodian jungle.

NOBODY WINS A WAR

Garry Trudeau, first comic-strip artist to win a Pulitzer prize for "best editorial cartooning" (1975) for his widely syndicated "Doonesbury," has zeroed in with equal abandon on targets both to the right and left. His "victims" include the semantic bull of all sides, press, activists and reactionaries, and such items as colonial attitudes, plant crazes, the Vietnam war, communes, media techniques, etc. Trudeau has also looked askance at his own contemporaries with a strange mixture of love, sadness and humor. "It's just possible that my peers will self-destruct," he has said. "How tragic the passing of this generation or at least their spirit, will be. I will lament because they are my contemporaries, my friends.

A Yale graduate and an intense admirer of Charles "Peanuts" Schultz, the late Walt "Pogo" Kelly," and Jules Feiffer, Trudeau's early efforts were contained in a comic strip called "Bull Tales" for Yale's *Daily News* in 1969. His work attracted the attention of young enterprising editors at the newly-formed Universal Press Syndicate who, sensing that perhaps the time was ripe for a change in the nation's comic pages, began selling an expansion of that same strip in 1970.

A far cry from the days of "Mutt and Jeff," "Bringing Up Father," and other original conceptions of the comic strip, a typical Trudeau cartoon might show the same view of the White House in each of its four panels.

DOONESBURY   by Garry Tru

A tremendous political consciousness and sense of social satire guides Garry Trudeau's facile pen as he takes the U.S. Secretary of the Treasury and Federal Energy Office "over the coals."

Here, the same TV set appears in each of Trudeau's panels, but the cartoonists's acerbic commentary keeps readers eyes from wandering to any other "channel" in their favorite newspaper.

©G.B. Trudeau, 1974, distributed by Universal Press Syndicate

Below, the panels again appear static, but close observation reveals that the characters portrayed keep changing and each is a separate study.

Incidentally, was the then energy chief William E. Simon bothered by the thinly-veiled spoof of himself? Nay, he even phoned Trudeau, begging for the original!

Edd Uluschak was born near Prosperity, Alberta, and is one of Canada's most widely syndicated cartoonists, with his work appearing not only in his own country, but abroad as well.

Winner of numerous citations, including the National Newspaper Award and the Basil Dean Memorial Award for outstanding contribution to journalism, he began to work for the Edmonton (Alberta) *Journal* in the late 1960's.

"We can finally keep up with the Joneses—he got laid off today."

From the mouth of babes: An Uluschak cartoon on one of the problems in war-torn Ireland.

"I don't think I'd make a good grown-up—I don't hate anybody."

In a lighter mood, the editorial cartoonist offers us these:

reciate your concern regarding too much violence on TV, ma'am but the program refer to as having reached a new high in savagery happened to be a newscast."

L.D. Warren began cartooning for the Camden (New Jersey) *Courier-Post* in 1926. Then came a tour of duty with the Philadelphia *Record*. Finally, in 1947, The Cincinnati *Enquirer* welcomed him to its pages and during the ensuing years Warren responded by garnering prizes for his work from the National Cartoonists Society, the National Conference for Christians and Jews, and many other organizations.

On the occasion of his retirement in 1973, the *Enquirer* stated editorially: "He has injected a ray of humor into otherwise solemn and portentous events. He has brightened the *Enquirer*'s editorial page and contributed very notably to this newspaper's stature and repute. He has put his talents to work on behalf of a vast range of humanitarian and philanthropic causes, and he has brought to himself and to the *Enquirer* an imposing array of citations and awards for his skill as well as his sound conceptions of citizenship."

Where Brotherhood Binds The Brave

'I Don't Care What the Lion Said! You Are White—With Black Stripes!'

Here is L.D. Warren on a variety of subjects.

On the ladies

DIRTY POOL

On something that could put us *all* behind the 8-ball.

'Disgustin'! Ain't It?'

DRAW YOUR OWN CONCLUSION

This was the final drawing of L.D. Warren in 1973, on the occasion of his official retirement.

Over a period of years, an editorial cartoonist tries almost every technique in drawing and just about every kind of art material available; also, he keeps increasing his range of interests until, indubitably, he qualifies as an elder statesman. That, in a nutshell, is the story of "L.D."

Clyde Wells began employment as editorial cartoonist for newspapers in 1971, after being a salesman and doing general art work and sports cartoons. He was born in Polk County, Florida, and attended schools in that state and in South Carolina.

Clyde Wells begins his day by showing editors several rough sketches of ideas, over which occasionally there is mild disagreement. He then does a finished drawing on two-ply Bristol board with a Staedter Mars technical pen, brushes, and whitener, and a screen for gray tones.

Hate-mongers might have been given cause to reflect by this drawing of a beloved statue slowly being reduced to rubble. Notice how the editorial cartoonist has drawn the lady standing proud and straight, as if she were still worth saving.

The proverbial house of cards, located at a well-known Washington, D.C. address. Wells has suggested in ink and wash that cold wintry winds had already laid bare the acreage on which it stands.

© Augusta Chronicle

"WELCOME ABOARD GERRY'. . .JUST DON'T ROCK MY BOAT."

Doug Wright was born in England and arrived in Canada while in his teens with a mother who longed to see him become a doctor, and two sisters. Stationed at Rivers, Manitoba, during the war, he became a cartoonist by accident when fellow air force recruits began laughing at his doodlings.

A cartoon strip, *Doug Wright's Family*, based on doings in his own household, and the average man's preoccupation with pot-holes, taxes, and other mundane problems, is published in Canada and syndicated all around the globe. One doesn't find politicians or public figures in Wright's work, but in the sense that this artist deals with the dilemma of people in a troubled society, he is "political."

"Doesn't matter who you vote for . . . they're all so busy primping to go on TV they don't have time to run the country!"

"I wish we could boycott food altogether! I just paid 49c for one onion!"

The high cost of living in Canada, helps Wright's readers identify with his work.

"There was a whole bunch of people here protesting about something . . . pollution, probably."

Ecological problems help the editorial cartoonist make contact with them, too.

"Don't nag ME about Safe Driving Week . . . I drive safely all year!"

Like his contemporaries in the States, Wright regularly carries on his own auto safety campaign.

Like many successful cartoonists, doing both editorial and comic art, Doug Wright began as a "ghost," helping the late Jimmy Frise with the strip *Juniper Junction,* then stepped out to try several features of his own. "The thing about this profession is, it's creative and rewarding," says Wright. "After all, in what other line, if a taxi driver cuts me off, could I get even with him in a drawing?"

Here, he examines patriotic fervor (?) in his own country.

"I wish they wouldn't telecast the National Anthem. I feel I ought to stand up!"

THE MODERNS/The World

EDITORIAL/POLITICAL CARTOONISTS ABROAD are like their fellow-professionals in the Western Hemisphere. They strive to be funny or serious, depending on the subject before them. And since social phenomena are so much the same everywhere nowadays, the overall result is a sort of *universality*.

EUROPE/*Austria*

This Austrian cartoon revealed Uncle Sam examining himself, on the occasion of President Kennedy's assassination.

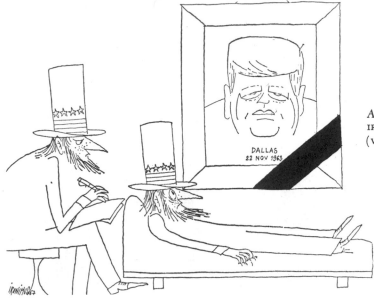

America on the couch
IRONIMUS iN DIE PRESSE
(VIENNA)

According to this Austrian cartoon, the U. S. press and the U.S. Senate were tearing President Nixon to shreds as he was meeting with Leonid Brezhnev.

HOW DO YOU DO?

Karikatur: „Die Zeit"/Mursch

EUROPE/*Belgium*

A Belgian cartoon by Picha, shows Uncle Sam sinking deeper and deeper into the inexorable mess of Indochina with every step he takes.

The split in the Catholic Church over marriage, as seen in Belgium, with a fine caricature of Pope Paul.

De Nieuwe Gazet

EUROPE/*Czechoslovakia*

Clever concept has the junta government in Chile, trying to build a new nation out of a prison foundation, in this cartoon from Czechoslovakia.

Rudé Právo

EUROPE/*East Germany*

East Berlin concept of life in the United States.

Eulenspiegel

EUROPE/*Finland*

In this amusing "three-panel" cartoon by Finland's Kari, a robber (inflation) defies a "Watch for the Angry Dog" sign, to approach a doghouse (government), and in the end finds no problem at all, naturally, because "it recognized me!"

Kari, copyright by arrangement with Helsingin

EUROPE/*France*

This cartoon satirizes the mod generation and is *funny*.

"I'm expecting friends ... Can't you clean yourself up a bit?"

This cartoon satirizes push-button generals and is *mad*.

Paris-Match

A funny French drawing on the subject of automation.

"I am your savior. If you would like to be saved,
put three nickels in the slot. I am your savior. . ."   Paris-Match

Inflation is universal and France has not escaped its effect, even though in this cartoon the reader might reasonably assume that the butcher was merely penalizing a slow customer.

"Alas, while you were pondering, the price of steak went up 50 cents."

France's Bernie sees his President enticing England into something of a trap, in this cartoon.

"WHO ME?...NO!...I AM NOT LIKE deGAULLE!"   Aux Ecoutes

Of course, in France they *do* know America has pollution. But doesn't *everybody?*

Le Canard Enchaîné

EUROPE/*Germany*

"It goes without saying that the Federal government is firmly convinced it will be able to regain control over the runaway inflation," reads the caption in this West German cartoon by Markus, featuring a couple of former heads of state: Chancellor Willy Brandt standing in front of brand new paper money bearing his own image and, on the phone, Minister of Finance Helmut Schmidt.

»Selbstverständlich rechnet die Bundesregierung fest damit, die galoppierende Inflation wieder in den Griff zu bekommen!«

"I think he's turned vegetarian," are the words NATO Secretary General Joseph Luns is hearing, as he rattles that collection box "For our Security," in a rendering by German cartoonist F. Behrendt.

„Ich glaube, er ist Vegetarier geworden"   Frankfurter Allgemeine Zeitung

"I know, historically speaking it's not authentic, but how else are we supposed to make a musical out of this?" asks German cartoonist Peter Neugebouer's movie director satirically, in this very effective wash drawing.

Peter Neugebauer

Adolf Hitler Superstar

»Ich weiß, es ist historisch falsch, aber wie sollen wir denn sonst ein Musical daraus machen?«

EUROPE/*Great Britain*

Great Britain's Prime Minister becomes "The Boy Who Cried Wolf," in this children's book-type illustration from *Punch*.

"Wolf! Wolf!"   © Punch

The same artist varies his style to offer a militaristic, if highly inept-looking, North Atlantic Treaty Organization war machine.

Sir Winston's utterance during World War II floats on the breeze, 'neath the White Cliffs of Dover, as English society tears itself apart in this *Punch* cartoon, done in still another style by Mahood.

"...WE SHALL DEFEND OUR ISLAND WHATEVER THE COST MAY BE, WE SHALL FIGHT ON THE BEACHES....."

Three whimsical comments on the social-political scene by England's Cookson.

"YE CAN NEVER BE SURE THESE DAYS, LADDIE. IT MAY BE ONLY A NEW OIL PIPELINE."

London Evening News

That well-known monster of Loch Ness comes in for close scrutiny here.

"It's a compromise—instead of torpedoes and missiles"

A suggestion on disarmament from the same cartoonist, who obviously remembers his boyhood.

The Queen herself appears in this faithful portrayal of both Her Majesty and that well-known doorway on Downing Street.

The cartoonist takes us on a Greek-island, Holy Land tour for three more of his comments.

"IT BEGAN AS A SECURITY IDEA YEARS AGO BUT NOW NOBODY CAN REMEMBER WHICH ONE IS THE REAL MAKARIOS."

We start out by seeing some finely drawn members of the Greek Catholic Church—

'There's nothing in the brochure about beach entertainment'

—thence to the once sun-kissed shores of Cyprus—

"YET LIVE IN HATRED, ENMITY AND STRIFE AMONG THEMSELVES, AND LEVY CRUEL WARS, WASTING THE EARTH, EACH OTHER TO DESTROY." JOHN MILTON 1608-1674.

—and, as the sun slowly sets in the Middle-East, we hear the immortal words of one of England's greatest poets

London Evening News

'And please God, let him win the election.'

'It's from a soldier in Belfast, saying "Wish you were here".'

'And for a keen young man the prospects of corruption are excellent.'

Two candidates for Prime Minister of Great Britain say their prayers in this preposterous cartoon by Jon.

Here the winner gets some "fan mail."

Jon's cynical view of politics might have struck a sympathetic chord among his readers.

A clue as to just how jolly things are these days in Jolly Old England is offered by the cartoonist here.

'Ten per cent. on petrol, have to sell the car.'

'Can't afford the new rail fares—no holiday.'

'Must give up smoking . . . and drinking.'

'Basic income tax up—postage up.'

'Another budget in the autumn.'

'I'll never last to be 65 and enjoy the increased pension.'

This splendid pen-and-ink drawings by Trog, in what might be called the classic *Punch* tradition, captures with humor and horror (for those fussy about their bedmates) the economic nightmare of Great Britain. The painstaking execution of that four-poster, the "situation" in which the beautiful lady finds herself, and the loathsomeness of her frog companion, add up to a one-two-three *smash*.

© Punch   . . . AND IN THE MORNING HE WAS STILL A FROG

In these three additional cartoons by Trog, we see that he subscribes to the large head–small body type of caricature discussed earlier in this book.

"QUICKLY, A NEW SABRE, EVEN IF IT'S JUST TO RATTLE!"

FREEDOM FIGHTERS

The Observer

The Trojan Horse theme has been used many times by editorial/political cartoonists, but executed freshly, as in this case by England's Waite, dealing with the situation in Cyprus, it is always welcome!

London Daily Mirror

A PRESENT FROM GREECE

Maps that dissolve into human forms have been used many times, too, but again showing his flair for updating, Waite eases the tension with this cartoon that appeared at a time when Irish "bomb letters" were arriving in his country.

"HELLO POLICE? I WISH TO REPORT
A SUSPICIOUS PARCEL....."

Altering his style, Waite dealt a double blow to polluters and public utilities in this amusing cartoon.

"I DON'T CARE HOW MUCH THE PHONE
BILLS ARE GOING UP, THIS IS A SMOKE-
LESS ZONE."

Ideas is the name of the game, and it isn't cartoonist Mac's fault that B.P. also stands for British Petroleum.

'I believe it stands for Big Profits.'

'Remember the old days when they used to come and take photographs of our beggars?'

The new-found affluence of the Arab world, is Mac's inspiration here.

In this cartoon, he echoes the frustration sentiments of his fellow professionals on the emergence of "hard-to-get" public figures.

"I BELIEVE THEY ARE CARTOONISTS, M'SIEU LE PRESIDENT."

DOCTOR WILSONSTEIN   London Daily Mail

Cynicism is the undeniable attitude of England's Emmwood.

Here Emmwood is cynical of the new government of Prime Minister Wilson.

Here he is cynical of certain governments abroad.

THE NEW REGIME

Here Emmwood is cynical of *almost* anything!

THE UNACCEPTABLE FACE OF POLITICS

Britain's Cookson and Trog twit a King-to-be, in these two cartoons.

"IS IT REALLY TRUE THAT ONE DAY ALL THIS WILL BE MINE?"

"I HOPE CHARLES DOES SOMETHING
SOON - I NEED ANOTHER ROYAL WEDDING!"

London Evening News

A panorama of Death, is the gruesome commentary on Cyprus, below, by Illingworth.

"But, gentlemen, the problem is settling itself..."

London Daily Mail

THE NEW IMPERIALISTS

England's Steadman is a bit dubious in this cartoon about that "giant step forward for mankind" mentioned by American astronaut Neil Armstrong.

In this one by Trog, a couple of old supremacists are deserted by a third, and left holding the coffin, so to speak.

"I'm inquiring about a bracelet I dropped overboard in 1937."

"We fed in all the facts—IRA, UDA, Brian Faulkner, Ian Paisley, Loyalists, bombers, anarchists, terrorists . . ."

In the great tradition of Gillray, Tenniel and Low, here are England's Audley and Cookson being *funny* and serious at the same time.

And that same country's Illingworth is not kidding around either as evidenced in this example of *his* work.

"The Pen Is Mightier . . ."

EUROPE/*Hungary*

Great cartoonist Ludas Maty keeps 'em laughing in Hungary, in spite of housing shortages and inadequate hospital service.

"Congratulations! Your wife has given birth to an apartment. . ."

A comment on the housing situation in Hungary, that might not have been amusing over there.

Ludas Matyi/Budapest

Hungarian concept of two major American political parties rolled into one.

LUDAS MATYI Budapest

EUROPE/*Ireland*

Irish Independent

Ireland's Doll sees one dead bird, and that's what we can see too, regretfully, in the northern part of his island.

Another Doll cartoon on Ireland that might conceivably make *any-body* go bananas.

Irish Independent

EUROPE/*Netherlands*

An effective comment on the same explosive situation, from Amsterdam by Behrendt.

END OF UNDERDEVELOPMENT.....

Het Parool

An Amsterdam view of the titanic struggle between the two Red powers, with neither of the adversaries resembling Groucho, Harpo, or Chico, in the eyes of cartoonist Behrendt.

EUROPE/*Norway*

A golden calf ascends the heights, in this cartoon from Norway by Hicks in *Die Welt*.

EUROPE/*Poland* ────────────────────

Funny Polish drawing of big business in distress.

ZBIGNIEW ZIOMECKI IN SZPILKI (WARSAW)

EUROPE/*Sweden*

Women's liberation is almost a universal movement. It certainly is making its influence felt in most European countries. Here is Saki of *Dagens Nyheter* of Stockholm, Sweden showing either how "it is" in that Scandinavian country or how it is about to be.

Saki/Dagens Nyheter/Stockholm

EUROPE/*Switzerland*

Die Weltwoche/Zurich

Here cartoonist Saver shows us how some people think of the "boob-tube" in Switzerland.

The link between the United States and Europe is extremely tenuous in this cartoon from Switzerland.

EUROPE/*Turkey*

A fine impressionist drawing from Turkey, demonstrating the slaying of an imperialist dragon at the hands of the Vietcong enemy.

A simply drawn Turkish cartoon by Turhan, showing all the alphabetical agencies of the United Nations in pompous display, blithely ignoring the disinherited of the earth bringing up the rear, with three pitiful letters of their own.

Turhan/Istanbul
"milliyet"

"No comment," says Olympic-style marathon runner Sadat, neatly side-stepping an effort to throw cold water on his political views, in this Turkish cartoon by Ali Ulvi.

YAZISIZ

Tazminat arttırılmazsa, haşhaş ekimine izin vereceğimizi Amerika'ya bildirdik.   — Basın —

HAYSİYETLİ DIŞ POLİTİKA

"Honorable Foreign Policy" is Ali Ulvi's title for the above, and he has the Turkish spokesman exclaiming, "we have informed America that if she doesn't increase our compensation for not planting poppies, then we shall give permission to plant them."

EUROPE/*U.S.S.R.*

Несмотря на позитивные сдвиги, происшедшие в международной обстановке за последнее время, на Западе еще есть силы, мыслящие категориями «холодной войны». Они выступают за продолжение гонки вооружений, противодействуют шагам на пути к миру.

Ковыляя в... прошлое.   **Рис. Гр. Оганова.**

This cartoon by G. Oganov in *Pravda* explains to Soviet readers that, in spite of positive trends in the international situation recently, there are still forces in the West thinking in terms of the "Cold War," coming out in favor of a continued arms race, and opposing steps leading to peace.

Another Russian cartoon, by M. Abramov, illustrates a statement of [the soon-to-be assassinated] President of Chile, Salvador Allende, urging that his government bring order into the economic and political sphere, and that it be prepared to defend that country.

Президент Чили Сальвадор Альенде подчеркнул, что правительство должно навести порядок в политической и экономической области, защитить Чили.   **(Из газет).**

Чили наводит порядок.   **Рис. М. Абрамова.**

Russian editorial cartoons frequently are accompanied by a "libretto." This one by V. Chernikov, from *Izvestiya*, entitled "Dividing the Cake," describes how "serious economic difficulties and intensification of the struggle for markets in the capitalist world are contributing to a further aggravation of relations among the three major centers of capitalist rivalry—the U.S.A., the Western European Countries of the Common Market, and Japan."

Серьезные экономические трудности, усиление борьбы за рынки в капиталистическом мире ведут к дальнейшему обострению отношений между тремя основными центрами капиталистического соперничества — США, западноевропейскими странами «общего рынка» и Японией.

Делят «пирог»... Рис. В. Черникова.

В издевательствах над коренным африканским населением и в попытках задушить патриотические движения — во всем этом режимы ЮАР и Родезии сотрудничают давно.

Два сапога — пара.   Рис. Д. Агаева.

This Russian cartoon, entitled "Two boots — one pair," by D. Agayev in *Sotsialisticheskaya Industriya* shows Prime Minister Vorster of South Africa and Prime Minister Smith of Rhodesia sharing the label "colonialism" imprinted on the soles of their boots.

The unmistakable hand of Uncle Sam holds the cracked Liberty Bell in this cartoon from *Izvestiya*, from which "refuse, science and ironic advice" are being disseminated.

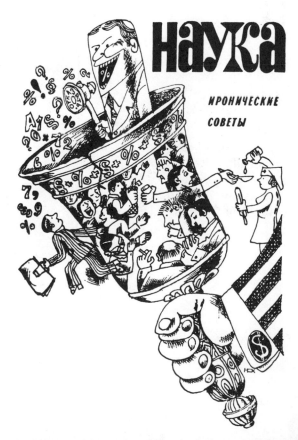

Цены в США на товары первой необходимости за последние годы стремительно подскочили вверх. Высокая стоимость жизни зажала в тиски миллионы американцев.

Рис. из американской газеты «Дейли уорлд».

In this American cartoon (reprinted in the Soviet *Krasnaya Zvezda*, from the *Daily World*,) we learn, if we didn't know it before, that prices in the U.S.A. on indispensable consumer goods have jumped considerably over the last year, and that the cost of living has gripped millions of Americans in a most formidable vise.

"Blue Daydream of Imperialist Reactionaries," is the translation of A. Zolotarev's cartoon on the subject of Cyprus.

«ГОЛУБАЯ МЕЧТА» ИМПЕРИАЛИСТИЧЕСКОЙ РЕАКЦИИ.

Рис. А. ЗОЛОТАРЕВА.

Врятувати СЕАТО — таке завдання черховодів, які намагаються замуровати тріщини в політичному фундаменті цього відмираючого агресивного блоку.

(З газет).

In the pages of *Radyanskaya Ukraina* (U.S.S.R.) appeared this cartoon by V. Petrenko, entitled "The Mender from SEATO," showing a junta "tailor" who has "received instructions from the bosses as they struggle to fix the cracks in the political foundation of this dying aggressive bloc."

Штопальник із СЕАТО.

Малюнок В. Петренка.

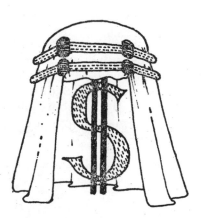

The mystery of what holds up an Arabian tent, is "solved" in this editorial/political cartoon.

"Bureaucracy" is seen as a place where one can really get a run-around, in this Russian cartoon.

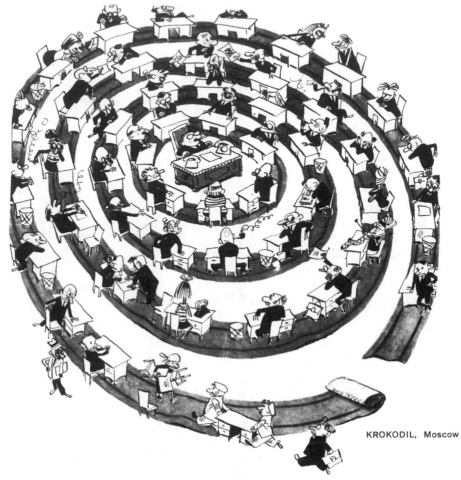

KROKODIL, Moscow

The work of three Soviet cartoonists, the "Kukriniksi" done in 1942 during World War II, prophetically showing German troops marching to their death.

This editorial cartoon from the Soviet Union is directed against the smog problem in a local area of that country.

Krokodil/Moscow

"Comrade Director, on the occasion of your anniversary, allow us to present you with a working model of your factory!"

Krokodil/Moscow

An amusing comment on the crime situation, from the Soviet Union.

"Why did you bring your wife?" "She's afraid to stay in the apartment alone at night."

fića

(KARIKATURA: M. DOBRIĆA)

The high cost of food is spoofed in M. Dobrica's cartoon from Yugoslavia, showing thieves bypassing a jewelry store in favor of swiping a couple of loaves of bread.

Another cartoon from the same country, spoofs inflation, with a merchant upgrading even his state of health.

A funny cartoon style helps this funny comment on inflation's effect on family life in Yugoslavia.

We live OK, it was difficult in the beginning, but later we got used to price increases.   **(KARIKATURA: M. DOBRIČA)**

THE TRANSFORMATION OF ALBANIA

A nice clean line drawing. (Notice the evolution of that mustache.)

MIDDLE EAST AND AFRICA/*Egypt*

وصـل نيكسـون أمس الى السـعودية

"Nixon arrived in Saudi Arabia yesterday," reads the caption in the above Egyptian cartoon by Salah Jaheen, who practically gives his readers a *photo* of the President and his Secretary of State.

The Egyptian news item cartoonist Salah Jaheen chose to have fun with in this cartoon was the story that stated "Prisons will today begin to allow the prisoners out to visit their families." Jaheen has a prisoner's family exclaiming, "Who told you that we want you to visit us?"

السجون تبـدأ اليوم اخراج المسـجونين لزيارة عائلاتهم

ــ ومين قال لهم اننا عايزينك تزورنا !!

MIDDLE EAST AND AFRICA/*Iraq*

In this carton from Baghdad the Arabs are being cajoled and threatened by the I.P.C., then coming up with a move of their own.

Dumped off an oil drum is the "bad guy" in this Iraqi view of the Mid-East situation, by cartoonist Georgi Chalukov.

This powerful Iraqi cartoon, by Besam Farag, employing a poster style familiar in many countries, illustrates a poem called "The Song of the Sun," by Pablo Neruda, and is entitled "The Oil—The Gun."

MIDDLE EAST AND AFRICA/*Israel*

Israeli editorial cartoonist Kirscher says it with another kind of fruit in the above.

Two recent stars of the international ballet, Golda Meir and Richard Nixon, neatly captured in action, by an Israeli caricaturist.

MIDDLE EAST AND AFRICA/*Jordan*

A nice loosely-drawn Jordanian cartoon has the Israelis threatening peace in the Mid-East, with only that star of David on the soldier's helmet to identify the culprit.

In a cartoon from Jordan, by Rabah we see the Arab King blowing away papers containing different problems, such as, "The Creation of a Palestinian Country"; "Suggestions"; Bargains"; "Surrenders."

MIDDLE EAST AND AFRICA/*Lebanon*

Lebanon cartoonist Melhem Emad's problem in this cartoon is, everytime, when some thousands demonstrate and ten fall, it is considered a crime. The bakery and garbage strikers and the students say, "He destroyed the country."

(Ed. note: The answer may be under that hat.)

"The prison is for men," says the spokesman in this cartoon by Lebanon's Sadek, which further explains: "Today there will be sentencing in the case of the officers of the Ex-Second Bureau."

In this cartoon by Melhem Emad from *Al-Hayat* of Lebanon, the leader of Al-Takadumi Al Isheraki party, Kamal Jumblatt, just returned from a visit to India, is subjected to powerful attractions from both domestic and foreign political forces.

The same Jumblatt, by the same cartoonist, in yogi pose this time, declaring that he needs two months to determine his situation with the government. "It is forbidden to pipe for two months," we are told.

MIDDLE EAST AND AFRICA/*Syria*

Al-Thora

"So you are the cause of starvation."

Putting the blame where it certainly doesn't belong, in a bitingly satiric pen and ink style drawing.

MIDDLE EAST AND AFRICA/*South Africa*

The World

A South African drawing joyously hails a new step toward racial equality.

"The show only lasts 10 minutes—they censored it themselves!"

In this cartoon from South Africa the artist comments on the pervasive censorship in the country.

FAR EAST AND AUSTRALIA/*Australia*

Bruce Petty, in the *Australian* sees—well, he sees the bottom falling out.

The Australian

Another clever concept, from Australia this time, shows a national health plan that's rather unstable.

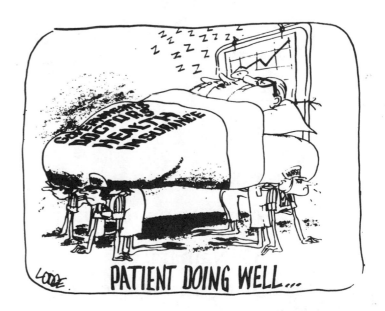

FAR EAST AND AUSTRALIA/*China*

This Chinese cartoon saw Lyndon B. Johnson and his Secretary of Defense good and stuck in the Far East.

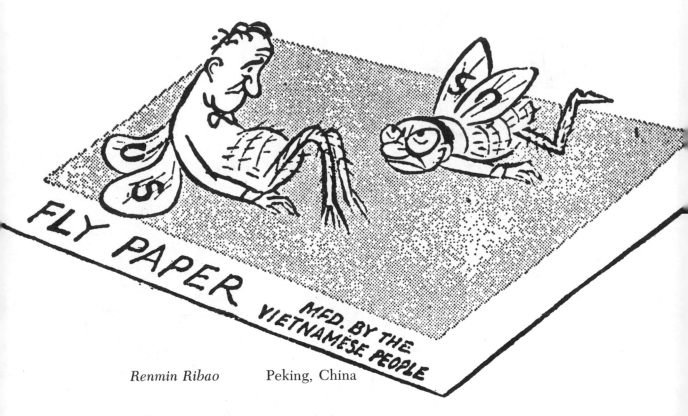

Renmin Ribao   Peking, China

Johnson:
"Any way out of this fix?"

McNamara:
"Bring in another 100,000 flies! How about it?"

FAR EAST AND AUSTRALIA/*India*

A bomb becomes the new deity, in this cartoon from India, by Abu.

Indian Express

Amusing cartoon of Mme Nehru and her cabinet on the run, for a pretty good reason.

FROM THE TIMES OF INDIA, Bombay

"I am sure the country is behind us."

FAR EAST AND AUSTRALIA/*Japan*

Japanese cartoonist Satoshi Imbashi offers readers this two-headed snake, the upper part designated "Provisions concerning the treatment of Heads of State," and the lower part marked "Lèse Majesté."

Hiroshi Ishiyama of Japan labels this cartoon "True partnership—never fearful, wincing, or hesitant." The caption over Nixon's sickle reads "Embargo on agricultural products"; while the one to the right of Kissinger reads "Jewish capital." The then Deputy Prime Minister of Japan, Takeo Miki (center) is sternly pointing to a document which says, "withdrawal from all occupied territories." The face on the floor, of course, is Israel's then Prime Minister Golda Meir, who might herself have been surprised at antisemitism in the Orient.

FAR EAST AND AUSTRALIA/*Philippines*

Real estate, art, industry—affluent Japanese were everywhere, buying *everything*, (on roller skates, yet!) as we see in this cartoon from the Philippines.

"Did I let him in?"
From THE MANILA BULLETIN, Manila

FAR EAST AND AUSTRALIA/*Singapore* _____

Historic patching up job done by Dr. Kissinger in the Mid-East (via a wounded camel) again shows the Western influence on cartooning.

Singapore Nanyanysiary

LATIN AMERICA/*Argentina*

A zany drawing to fit a zany joke from Argentina.

"Was the coup against the government?"
"Which government?"

El Mundo

LATIN AMERICA/*Brazil*

Brazil's Zélio presents U.S. Secretary of State Henry Kissinger involved in a tug-of-war between the Arabs and Israel, remarking "Damn it! What a lack of imagination. ."

Cartoonist Biganti's "Long Hours of Negotiation," from the same country, showed the same Secretary of State rushing to give Richard Nixon a peace treaty that was signed by Syria and Israel, and modestly allowing the President to take credit for it.

Longas horas de negociações

LATIN AMERICA/*Colombia*

From Colombia, South America, we get this nightmarish concept of "WAR," by Gonzalo Angarita, hardly about to come to a halt, in spite of that little character on the right holding up his hand so meaningfully.

Here Angarita shows that even the anti-pollution groups resort to pollution devices to get across their message.

ANGARITA

LA ADHESION FEMENINA   —   Por Luisö

From Colombia comes "The feminine adherence," with Latin America in Luise's cartoon, remarking, "Doctor, women's support is quite obvious."

—Mi doctor, se nota bastante el respaldo femenino....

YA NO RESISTE   —   Por Luisé

Hay que aumentar impuestos

"It can't be endured any longer," says Luise's caption here. "Taxes must be increased." And, sure enough, it's blood they're squeezing out of the poor guy in this cartoon!

LATIN AMERICA/*Cuba*

La atmósfera capitalista está cargada

"The capitalistic influence is getting dark," is *Gramma's* title for this cartoon from Havana, Cuba, on the subject of inflation and high prices for the average consumer in that country.

Another *Gramma* cartoon, entitled "Supercynicism," shows a trio of villainous foreigners with Castro in tow, informing him, "we accuse you of treason to the Motherland."

EL SUPERCINISMO

U.S. embassies in Latin America   Hoy

LATIN AMERICA/*Mexico*

"Is the wealthier class doing its share of carrying the burden?" we are asked in this cartoon by Vadillo, from Mexico.

Vadillo - Siempre, Mexico

The same cartoonist gives us a preview of what might happen if a certain class ever gets tired of doing *all* the carrying.

RIUS IN SIEMPRE! (MEXICO CITY)

An excellent Mexican pen and ink study of the contrast in upper and lower class society, with the fate of both apparently depending on the latter.

In this cartoon the artist suggests that Nixon himself "axed" Spiro Agnew.

El Universal

The insidious hand (and feet) of the Central Intelligence Agency is seen in this Mexican cartoon.

El Universal

One little push was all we needed, according to a Mexican observer.

Vadillo in *Siempre* leaves no doubt as to who suffered during Chaplin's banishment by the United States.

CHAPLIN

Siempre

LATIN AMERICA/*Peru*

"Even with X-Ray," says this Lima, Peru, cartoon by Asdrubal, and of course it refers to the perspiring Mr. Nixon and some White House tapes the harried President might have tried swallowing.

HASTA CON RAYOS X

Asdrúbal

LATIN AMERICA/*Venezuela*

South American comment on the war in Southeast Asia, displays a, perhaps, well-deserved cynicism and fair amount of grotesqueness.

Bohemia

ALPHABETICAL LIST OF CARTOONISTS